BENNY GREEN

THE RELUCTANT ART

*

FIVE STUDIES IN THE GROWTH OF JAZZ

EXPANDED EDITION

A DA CAPO PAPERBACK

TO MY FATHER

EASILY THE BEST MUSICIAN

IN THE FAMILY

Library of Congress Cataloging-in-Publication Data

Green, Benny, 1927-
    The reluctant art : five studies in the growth of jazz / Benny
Green. -- Expanded ed.
        p.   cm. -- (A Da Capo paperback)
    Reprint. Originally published: London : MacGibbon & Kee,
1962. With new pref. and chapter.
    ISBN 0-306-80441-7
    1. Jazz--History and criticism. 2. Jazz musicians. I. Title.
ML3506.G73 1991
781.65'09--dc20   91-20307
                                                                  CIP
                                                                  MN

This Da Capo Press paperback edition of Benny Green's *The Reluctant Art* is an unabridged republication of the edition published in London in 1962, with the addition of a new preface by the author, and a chapter on Art Tatum originally published as liner notes to a boxed set of his recordings in 1976. This book is reprinted by arrangement with the author.

Published by Da Capo Press, Inc.
A Subsidiary of Plenum Publishing Corporation
233 Spring Street, New York, N.Y. 10013

CONTENTS

PREFACE
TO THE DA CAPO EDITION

THE Reluctant Art was twenty-eight books ago. It was the first book I ever wrote, and, being the first-born, retains my allegiance in the face of all its imperfections. At the time I wrote it, I was still very much a working jazz musician, playing the saxophone in a style loosely designated at the time as Modern. Today I still play, as a hobby, and it is indicative of the continuing hysterical pace of the evolution of the music that over a period of thirty years, without myself changing, I have regressed from the avant garde to the last ditch without ever experiencing any sensation of movement.

When I began writing this book, I had intended it to be at least twice as long. There was going to be a long analytical chapter on Coleman Hawkins to balance the one on Lester Young. There was going to be a disquisition on Artie Shaw, Shaw in those years being a much maligned man accused of not playing jazz by those odd folk, the commentators, who loved jazz with a passion so fierce that it was so very nearly but not quite fierce enough for them to learn how to play something. There was to be a section on Duke Ellington's orchestral technique, another on the universality of Louis Armstrong, another on the eclecticism of Art Tatum. I never wrote any of them. One day I just happened to meet a publisher's editor who offered me a £50 advance, so I took the money and ran. Later, when I had learned a little of the ways of publishing, I resolved to seek out my benefactor and confront him with his own chicanery. But when I went looking for him, I found that he had long forsaken the intellectual life for the simpler pleasures of running someone's restaurant. I don't think he ever read the book.

I remember that it was on the whole rather well received, except for some noodle in *down beat* who castigated me for having the presumption to write about Lester Young when I was too young to have been there when Lester was in the Basie band, although the entire content of the magazine appeared to consist of pieces by men who were, it seemed, too young to have been anywhere when anyone was with anybody. Whatever my shortcomings as an essayist, I certainly knew Young's playing better than anyone else writing on jazz, which is not saying much. The famous two choruses of improvisation on "Lady Be Good" with which Lester made his astonishing recording debut in 1936 so overwhelmed me with their beauty and startling originality that I resolved to con them by rote, and then, when I was note-perfect, go out into the musical world and amaze everyone I played with. That will give you some idea how unworldly I was at nineteen. I duly learned the solo by heart and unveiled it at a Jewish wedding in the East End of London when part of an execrable trio consisting of piano, electric guitar and yours truly. I played Lester's two sublime choruses with perfect accuracy to an audience too preoccupied with dyspepsia and old family scores to listen very carefully, only to realize as I reached the last cadence that I had performed the whole thing two beats in front of my fellow-impostors. But I was an innocent, tremulous beginner back then; it was thirty years before it dawned on me that in view of my expertise in playing the solo, it was probably the other members of the trio who were two beats behind.

The essay on Bix in particular was regarded as heretical in 1962, received opinion in those days being that Bix had sold his jazz birthright for a mess of Paul Whiteman's potage. Only someone who has never lived the musical life could ever believe such twaddle, and it gave me great pleasure to square the account. Today of course, all my views on Bix would be regarded as old hat by younger students of the music. I am only sorry that at the time the book was published, I did not know that among the several inconsistencies about that charming but doomed young man, was his ability to quote whole pages verbatim from the works of P.G. Wodehouse.

The only other memory roused from its torpor by the republication of this book is that one of its subjects read the chapter about himself so closely, and with such wonderful blockheadedness, that he spent the rest of his life sedulously avoiding me. Some years after the book was published in New York, Benny Goodman arrived in London, and among his engagements was a television interview by the musician-commentator considered to be the great expert on his style, yours truly. Goodman hastily backed off, telling the producer of the program that "Mr. Green does not understand the predicament of the American musician." I agreed to tear up my contract, more than consoled for the loss by the knowledge that Goodman had inadvertently endorsed my *bona fides*, for there is no finer testimony to a man's character than that Goodman should have disapproved of it.

For the rest, the book remains a statement of my views and a disclosure of my literary style half a lifetime ago. I have altered nothing, corrected nothing, preferring instead the evidence that in the last thirty years I have made certain small advances, as well as being presented with them by a succession of publishers. The only addition to the original text is an essay on Art Tatum written to accompany the appearance of Tatum's monumental twelve-album piano solo series recorded for Norman Granz. In the normal way of things, liner notes bear not the slightest resemblance to literature for the same reason that menu definitions have nothing to do with the quality of the food. In both cases the pressure of vested interests causes the literary sensibility to buckle. However, as I have never discerned any breach in

Tatum's armor, and have never been able to think of anything even faintly derogatory to say about it, the liner notes comprise a sort of essay after all.

BENNY GREEN
London
May 1990

THE RELUCTANT ART

1

'WHY RELUCTANT?'

MUSIC does not come out of the ether, it has to be conceived and performed by musicians. This is a very unfashionable view in the jazz world, where thousands of people spend their entire lives shoring up the walls of the romantic legend of jazz, pasting over the cracks in those walls which must inevitably be made by the long-range guns of reality. The legend, of course, is very attractive and takes more than one form. For instance, it can be Jazz as the Bawdy Musical Expression of Nonconformity, or Jazz as the Great Artistic and Intellectual Significance of Our Time. On the face of it this may appear strange, because the first version contradicts the second. But this, after all, is the very essence of legend, whose irresistible attraction lies in its independence of the commonplace rules of logic. Galatea may change into a woman and Dionysus into a ram without upsetting in the slightest the reader who approaches these metamorphoses in the appropriate spirit, and by the same token John Lewis may change into an Oracle and Mezz Mezzrow into Pure Fiction without causing much bewilderment in the spectators. Unfortunately the working musician rarely has much time for such diverting sport and has to face the realities of his profession as best he can.

Those realities are hard and uncompromising, and revolve around a single familiar pivot, which is that most people have

13

neither the time nor the temperament to interest themselves in what he is doing. They may embrace the trappings of his world as part of a social cult. They may cherish his music as a private, entirely subjective world of their own, unconsciously using the jazz they hear as the incidental music to a Proustian reconstruction of their own lives. They may support his efforts as part of their sociological homework. But only rarely are they inclined to trouble themselves to discover very much about the music itself and why it sounds the way it does. To most people the evolving styles of jazz occur with the same inevitability as the hands moving slowly around a clockface, and if some explanation must be provided, it usually has something to do with a magical aesthetic Life Force thrusting the musician onward and upward to artistic achievements over which he has little or no control.

The attitude of the musician towards this outside world with which he has somehow to come to terms, usually takes one of three forms. Either he is amused, or he is disgusted, or he believes what people tell him about himself. The first reaction gives us the high comedy of the hipster abroad in a world of dullards, the second the belligerence and pathos of the seeker after cheap euphoria, while the third establishes nebulous messiahs who come to regard the music they play as a kind of free pass into the pantheon of great art.

Now there is one way in which Jazz really is the most astonishing of all the arts, invaluable to the student of the artistic process, and that is the highly pressurized rate of its evolution. Jazz music has moved from Primitivism to Neo-Classicism within the space of half a century, and so, just as geneticists may breed a thousand generations of insects to study the effect of environment on hereditary tendencies, so the documentor of art may make a detailed study of jazz and note the effect of economic pressures on the nuances of instrumental thought.

This hypothetical observer will discover a certain disarming *naïveté* about jazz. He will find that it came into the world conceived in such complete cultural innocence that it never even knew it was a form of artistic expression at all. He will find that even today few people in the jazz world have really got over the joke. For the jazz musician, groping and stumbling forward in his quest for articulate expression, has been rather like a shipwrecked man who, knowing nothing of life on the mainland, slowly and painfully evolves his own primitive kind of alphabet, and is so elated after years of struggle to discover words of two syllables that he sincerely believes he has made a significant step forward on behalf of civilization. And, indeed, how can we laugh at him? He has performed a prodigious feat, and to belittle him because he has not yet evolved the sonnet form or mastered the subtleties of Irony would be most uncharitable.

That is why the terms employed in jazz criticism apply only in their own context, in the same way as the literacy of our islander only remains literacy by the standards of the island. The modernism of jazz is not modernism at all to anybody with a reasonable knowledge of nineteenth century music. It is merely called modern to mark the point in the evolution of jazz when one of its few real geniuses made the giant step from diatonic to chromatic harmony. In that sense only is the jazz of Charlie Parker modern.

There have been a few men who played similar roles to Parker. For various reasons these men found the conventions of their day inadequate, and attempted to break new ground. Sometimes their reasons were not purely musical. Sometimes they were not the outstanding musicians of their time. Nobody would pretend, for instance, that my inclusion of Benny Goodman in this collection and my omission of Louis Armstrong implies a belief that Goodman was a greater jazz musician than Armstrong. Some artists, and Armstrong is one of them, produce art so indigenous to their own spirit that it never occurs to them to change or evolve in any way. They create masterpieces so daunting that those who follow them are impelled to break away from the pattern and find something of their own. Which brings us to the second of the two huge jokes of jazz history, its relentless advance towards respectability.

As jazz advances technically, as it assimilates harmonies more and more complex, as it absorbs rhythmic variations that would have whitened the hair of the primitives of New Orleans, as it takes Chromaticism in its stride without strangling itself, it also advances socially, from the brothel to the ginmill to the dance hall to the concert stage and the cultural festivals of the world. Of course the music itself lost its innocence a long time ago, perhaps in the ballrooms of the Roosevelt era. But its practitioners still wrestle manfully with the terrifying problem of keeping alive the earthy spark of its beginnings. And every time somebody introduces a new harmony into the jazz context, then the task becomes more difficult.

For the production of valid jazz depends on a delicate compromise between acute awareness and complete unselfconscious ease, between extreme artistic agility and consummate relaxation. A jazz musician is a juggler who uses harmonies instead of oranges. So long as he limits himself to the ensemble techniques of early New Orleans he is being very spectacular about throwing and catching the lone orange of dominant-to-tonic discord and resolution. Each time he throws up an additional orange, it becomes increasingly difficult for him to achieve that relaxed poise of the spirit without which no jazz is worth the playing. No matter how dexterous he may be, he will become a bore if his preoccupation with the oranges destroys the charm of his movements and the grace of his attitude. Today our modernists are striving so hard that the air is thick with flying oranges, many of which fall to earth and trip up the juggler.

Jazz criticism often tends to place importance on the wrong aspects of this juggling act. Mr Balliet tells us how the oranges often appear to him as light brown or deep purple in colour. M. Hodeir calculates the velocity and rate of acceleration of the oranges, and then selflessly credits the musicians with a mathematical subtlety which they do not possess. M. Pannassie insists that once the number of oranges passes a limit set by himself, all the oranges cease to exist altogether. For the juggler it remains a tortuous affair. But a few valiant spirits still manage to perform fantastic feats of skill. And they have the questionable compensation of knowing that the background against which they perform their art gradually becomes better upholstered, better ventilated and better patronized as time goes on.

Whether this is really what the jazz musician wants I do not know, because he can be just as insufferable about the glories of the ginmill as he sometimes is about the kudos of the concert hall. But whatever his feelings about the daunting responsibility of the Creative Artist where once there was only the kick of having a blow, the handful of musicians who changed his situation either musically or socially or both at the same time, either deliberately or accidentally, either for better or for worse, are in some ways the most fascinating and significant figures on the entire jazz landscape.

2

BIX BEIDERBECKE

'... which is the right man,
Walt Whitman or Paul Whiteman? ...'

COLE PORTER

THE curse of jazz music is its hagiography, perhaps only to
be expected in an art form possessing so much surface flam-
boyancy. The apparent glory of the spectacle of a lone soloist
pitting his inventive powers against the world every time he
stands up to play, combined with the element of the picaresque in so many gifted musicians, has been the supreme mis-
fortune of the music. Popular journalism has found it easy
to tack on to the body of jazz a spurious romanticism tending
to obscure the art that lies beyond. There has been a surfeit
of what Walter Sickert once called 'the recourse to melodrama
to which the disinclination for real critical work drives some
critics'.

Not all the journalism was meant to have this effect. Some
of the very worst critics had the very best intentions. The
effect has been deadly nonetheless. Artistic prowess has been
neglected in favour of what the twentieth century refers to as
'human interest', a phrase which implies that poking one's
nose into other people's business is more edifying than poking
one's soul into other people's art.

Now the effect of magnifying the artist's personal foibles

at the expense of his creative output is to create a sourceless mythology, an order of saints without divine inspiration of any kind, which is precisely what has happened to jazz all through its history, and precisely why the world at large is consistently baffled by the spectacle of a bohemia seemingly peopled only by eccentrics and degenerates producing music which doesn't sound like music at all. It is as though for every genuine lover of painting there were fifty who knew only that Toulouse-Lautrec frequented bawdy houses.

That Buddy Bolden should be immortalized as a barber and scandalmonger whose trumpet could be heard at a range of one, five or ten miles, depending on the degree of fanaticism to which one adheres to his particular legend, is understandable, for no recordings of Buddy Bolden exist. That Freddie Keppard should be remembered for covering his trumpet valves with a handkerchief to hide his fingerings from covetous rivals is a little less sane, though it may well be aesthetic justice. That Frank Teschmaker should be mourned as an incipient genius cut down by a premature death is hardly acceptable in the light of his recorded work. That Lester Young should be deified as The Man in the Pork-Pie Hat and Charlie Parker fondly recollected as an attempted suicide is quite unforgivable, for by now the legend is devouring the art from which it sprang.

With Bix Beiderbecke the position is already impossible. Sanity long ago fled in wild disorder from the task of interpreting his career. The damage was done many years ago by two agencies, the mawkish contemporaries who grabbed prestige from accidental associations with him, and the disgracefully inept journalism over the years which encouraged the process because it made what was called 'very good copy', which always means very bad copy. Bix is jazz's Number One Saint, and any attempt at a rational analysis of his talent usually invokes the bitterness of a theological dispute.

THE RELUCTANT ART

Today Bix is a kind of patron saint of Improvisation, a
beatific figure before whom the idolators kneel in reverence,
and at whom the debunkers heave giant brickbats. Of course
the circumstances were ideal for this process of deification.
The exquisite talent, the weakness for bathtub gin, the
seraphic smile, the artistic frustration, the premature death,
all played out against the backdrop of the Roaring Twenties.
The façade has been building up, brick upon critical brick
over the years, until today the man is equated with all kinds
of people, objects and causes with which he has only the most
tenuous connections. Today, when anybody mentions Bix
Beiderbecke, a confused vision is conjured up of all the
variegated symbols with which he has been juxtaposed, from
Capone to Gatsby, from the crude fact to the artistic synthesis
of the fact. The dismal truth awaiting the earnest student of
Bix is that his vision will become impaired the moment
he breathes Bix's name, and that instead of one figure he will
see half a dozen, all interesting enough, but only one of which
has much to do with music. The five spurious Beiderbeckes
feed on the single reality, the hard core at the heart of the
myth, the creative artist. There is the cardboard martyr of the
Bixophiles who concoct biographies with acknowledgments
to the Princeton dance programmes of the Jazz Age; there is
the marvellous boy one critic talked of 'with wisps of genius
swirling around in his brain'; there is the whimsy-whamsy
superman of the Condon–Carmichael anecdotes; there is the
baby-faced apotheosis of the Jazz Age, with glib parallels
drawn between the Bix Crash and the Wall Street Crash—
'. . . like the stock markets, he was riding high but shake by
1929'; there is the actual jazz musician, the one-sixth of the
legend which has supported the parasitic growth of the other
five-sixths; and, finally, and in some ways the most fascinating of all facets of the legend, there is the fictive Bix pro-
jected by Miss Dorothy Baker in her novel *Young Man With*

a Horn, a book so perfectly symptomatic of the failure of the writer of fiction to perceive the quintessence of the Jazz Life that the discrepancies between it and the reality of Bix's experience should serve as an invaluable guide to the aspiring writer of jazz fiction. Fragments of the Bix myth are quite true of course. Bix Beiderbecke really is a key figure in the development of jazz. His dilemma really was a new one for the improvising musician, and he really was the first, perhaps the only, white musician to contribute something completely original to the jazz art which was not artistically suspect. Digesting the bare facts of his life one is soon convinced of the peculiar lovability of this amiable goofer Bix Beiderbecke, with his frightful *naïveté* in a worldly environment and his helplessness or irresponsibility which made a man like Frank Trumbauer desire to father him even at the expense of his own career. But Bix offered up as a martyr on the altar of fine art is more difficult to swallow. Bix's death, by no means the outcome of a self-destructive lust, seems rather to have been, like everything else in his life except his music, a confused accident, the aimless drift of an unsophisticated young man who was hardly aware at any time, of what was happening to him.

There were huge blanks in his musical education, and he evidently became increasingly aware of them. He must also have realized the comic ineptitude of many of the musicians with whom he worked. No great jazz musician ever kept worse musical company than Bix Beiderbecke. He seems to have spent most of his career working with lame dogs and most of his energies in helping them over a style. This apparent indifference to the poor quality of his companions is one of the surest indications of his amazing lack of awareness as a creative artist. To him, the dedicated ruthlessness of the creator would have seemed mere churlishness. Pee-Wee Russell once said, 'His disposition wasn't one to complain. He wasn't able to say, "I don't like this guy, let's give him the gate and get so-and-so". He was never a guy to complain about the company he was in.' It is in that last sentence of Russell's, and not in the idiotic talk of selling his soul to Paul Whiteman, that the only real indictment of Bix lies. 'He was never a guy to complain of the company he was in'. No more deadly accusation could be levelled at any artist.

Sensational as Bix's arrival must have seemed to those who witnessed it, it is clear on reflection that nothing could have been more inevitable. Of all the things that had to happen to jazz, Bix had to happen to it more certainly than all the others, and when jazz has finally run its course and its development seen for what it is, a single continuous process, even the time at which he appeared will seem to have been predictable almost to the year. The jazz Bix heard as a boy was born of a sociological phenomenon whose total effect on the history of man has yet to be charted. Jazz was the musical expression of an oppressed minority dumped on an alien society, and in its beginnings was therefore not respectable, certainly not to the kind of middle-class immigrants the Beiderbeckes typified.

By the time Bix was old enough to understand what he was hearing, jazz had already begun its advance north. He was only one of thousands of white youths intrigued by it. And just as surely as jazz was the result of the transference of African native culture into the melting pot of the Deep South, so was the Bixian dilemma of the last years born of the contrast between the hybrid music Bix played and the sensibilities of the essentially European mind which conceived that music, for although Bix is always nominated as the All-American Boy of his period (the notes to the Memorial album on American Columbia begin 'The Bix Beiderbecke Story is the great romantic legend of American jazz'), Bix was the son of German immigrants aware of European music who tried to school the boy in what they thought they knew.

There is indeed a sense in which Bix was a martyr, but it has nothing to do with all the puerilities about marijuana nights and bathtub gin. Bix was the first jazz musician who felt obliged to attempt a widening of the harmonic scope of jazz by grafting on to it some of the elementary movements of modern harmony, the first improviser to try to take the patterns beyond the primitive shapes of New Orleans and give them a tint of the subtleties of the Impressionist composers of Europe.

By the end of his short life he had become less interested in the cornet, and obsessed instead by the piano and the half-formulated pieces he composed for it, a change of attitude with the most profound implications. The added harmonic dimensions of the piano, on which he was able to strike several notes simultaneously, were obviously better suited to his purpose. By that time the early days with the Wolverines only seven years before, days when he was a mere boy carrying the entire band on his shoulders, must have seemed far distant indeed, uncomplicated days before his own developing sensibilities forced him far beyond the point for which his training and experience had equipped him.

The body of legend dimly appreciates that a tension of this kind existed somewhere in Beiderbecke's life, but interprets it with unfailing lack of perception. The Bix legend goes very briefly as follows—'Innocent young white boy with jazz gift. Becomes recognized and records masterpieces in the Big City. Starts to drink. Reaches peak around 1927. Sells his soul to commercialism. Falls ill. Half-recovers. Dies. End of life, beginning of legend.' It will be perceived that this framework leaves convenient gaps for the insertion of gangsters, the Right Woman, the Wrong Woman and the rest of the clumsy farrago which takes the music for granted and delivers a kind of affectionate rap on Bix's posthumous knuckles for being naughty enough to join a band as corrupted as Paul

Whiteman's, a band whose only contribution to jazz was the money it poured into the pockets of those who sat in its elephantine ranks.

This artistic defection of Bix's is the one big blot on his copybook, the sole act for which posterity finds it difficult to forgive him. Indeed some criticism cannot find the heart to forgive him at all, being possessed of no heart in the first place, nor a brain nor an ear. Rudi Blesh once wrote with tight-lipped resolution, 'Bix's playing is weak. He just pretended to be a jazz musician because his weakness permitted him to play in the commercial orchestras of Whiteman and Jean Goldkette. Bix was neither a tragic nor an heroic character, he was a figure of pathos.' Leaving aside the curious defective logic of Blesh's second sentence, I am obliged to admit that there is a whole school of this criticism which discounts Bix, and throughout this school great stress is laid on the fact that Bix finally went for the fleshpots when he should have been preserving his innocence.

Now this kind of plot stands up very well when it is transferred to an idiom as crass as itself, for instance Hollywood and the fourpenny library romantics. But as an evaluation of Beiderbecke the artist it is so wildly inept that no deliberate parody of authentic criticism could ever get further from the mark. The truth about what happened to Bix and the motives behind his apparently irresponsible behaviour are obvious to any thinking jazz musician who has himself experienced, even if to a far less vital degree, the process which took hold of Beiderbecke. Educated by his own worldly experience as an artist, the jazz musician looks at the great mound of rubbish which has accumulated about Bix's figure and chuckles in wonder to himself, thinking perhaps that after all it is hardly reasonable to expect much better from such a parcel of fools.

The Artist-Who-Sold-His-Soul-For-A-Hip-Flask theory

is useful in one way, because it is so completely, utterly hopelessly wrong that all one has to do to get to the truth of the
matter is to reverse all its main propositions. After all, the
man who is consistently wrong is just as sure a guide to con-
duct as the man who is consistently right.

The one significant thing about Bix is not that he sold his
soul to Paul Whiteman for three hundred dollars a week, but
that he refused to sell his soul, no matter what the consequences, and that he would have been prepared to sacrifice
everything, even the one priceless gift he possessed, his jazz
gift, rather than compromise musically so much as a semi-
quaver. The conventionally accepted story of Bix's growing
artistic lassitude which finally destroyed him, may be neatly
reversed to arrive at the truth. Bix embodies the case of
artistic irresponsibility and unawareness which imperceptibly
evolves into a growing wonder at the glory of music and a
desperate attempt to create something worthy of that glory.
It is a process half-aesthetic, half-intuitive, and all the more
peculiar for the fact that throughout his adult years Bix
remained intellectually unaware of the process that had taken
hold of him, unable to rationalize its effects, unable to help
the process along, unable even to opt out for the simple
reason he was hardly aware he had ever been opted in. Iain
Lang struck miles nearer the target than Blesh when he remarked that there was no hard core of intelligence or character in Bix to enable him to cope with his unwieldy fame,
although he too goes on to describe the Whiteman episode
as a compromise.

What did, in fact, happen to Bix had to happen to somebody as soon as jazz started to travel north into the nation at
large where middle-class whites like Bix could hear it and be
stirred by it. About Bix's reaction to the tremendous strains
imposed upon him by his unique experience at the hands of
music, there is something which borders, not on the heroic,

25

but on the comic, and the fact that neither intellectually nor morally was he equipped to cope with that experience does make some belated sense out of Blesh's word 'pathetic'. The most comical thing of all about this battered reputation of Bix Beiderbecke is that there is little opposition to the Sale-of-Soul theory. Instead of opinion being divided between the Bleshes on one hand, who believe that as Bix knew he couldn't play jazz anyway, he joined the highest-paid band in the country and made the best financially out of his own shortcomings, and those like myself who can see quite clearly that joining Whiteman was artistically the only honest thing Bix could possibly have done, the field is divided between those who know Bix joined Whiteman and despise him for it, and those who know he joined Whiteman and forgive him for it. Both the Bixophobes and the Bixophiles miss the point.

★ ★ ★

In 1923 a band called the New Orleans Rhythm Kings was playing in Chicago. It was the first important white band in jazz history and it was among those which brought to Chicago the authentic source-music of New Orleans. Bix Beiderbecke, enrolled at a nearby military academy for the sons of middle-class families, spent his week-ends listening to them. By the end of the year, he was already propping up his comrades in the Wolverines, the first white band to be composed wholly of non-New Orleans musicians. These 'firsts' are more important than they might appear to the casual reader, for they chart minutely the spread of jazz across the Continent. The Rhythm Kings were significant because they were the first convincing proof (with apologies to the Original Dixieland Jazz Band) that white musicians could generate effectively the spirit of jazz. And the Wolverines were just as significant because they proved, though far less effectively, that this spirit could be acquired at second-hand, that jazz was not

26

merely a local dialect, but that those with a sympathy for it and some musical endowment might come to acquire its nuances. The New Orleans Rhythm Kings and the Wolverines are the first and second premises in the proof of the proposition that jazz, like more formal kinds of music, is universal.

The incident of the young Beiderbecke catching up with the rare spectacle of the Rhythm Kings in full cry is not so extraordinary. There were thousands like Bix who sensed that something unusual had happened to music. For those thousands, the piquancy of the experience must slowly have faded away, finally achieving the status of an adolescent love affair, as indeed it was in a way, fondly but faintly remembered. Bix did not react in this way for the very good reason that he was abnormal. Perhaps only slightly so, but enough to transform what was for others a casual incident on the road to maturity into an event of shattering import. Bix was that rare bird, the natural or born musician, the kind who unnerves the layman when he reads about him and tempts him to embrace half-baked theories of reincarnation or demoniac possession to explain away his own mediocrity. Bix's musical gift as a small child even won a brief local fame. His mother later said that at three years he could pick out with one finger on the piano the melody of Liszt's Second Hungarian Rhapsody. Later the Davenport press referred to 'this prodigy who at seven could play any selection he heard'.

We now come to the first significant point in Bix's development. An attempt was made at formal musical instruction. The attempt failed. It failed because, as George Hoefer wrote in one of the few rational essays on Bix which exist, 'The teacher gave up, realizing he couldn't teach the boy anything and that the talent was one which lay deep within'. In fact, time was to prove that it lay so deep within that nobody, Bix included, ever really succeeded in digging it out.

Now the failure at formal instruction represents the kind of impasse which is reached in almost all attempts of parents to educate their children musically. The comedy of the Piano Lesson looms large in the childhood of countless people whose musical potential proved to be negligible. Someone notices in a child what he thinks is an obvious gift for music, at which the middle-class vision sees the concert halls of Europe, tailcoats and floral tributes. The lessons, if they are given at all, are usually given very badly, and the collapse of the scheme quickly follows, bringing down with it whatever might have been of the original talent. The precosity is half-forgotten and over the years is gradually reduced to the proportions of a family reminiscence. . . . '. . . you should have heard Bixie when he was a kid. Play anything and couldn't read a note. That kid really had an ear for music. . . .'

As it happened, Bixie had more than just an ear for music, he had something much more serious, a soul which hungered for it. Evidently when the teaching began, Bix was too young and too immature to sense any dynamic in what he was being shown, but in his teens he had a fresh encounter with music in the one form capable of galvanizing him into positive action. He needed something bright and gaudy to attract his adolescent sensibilities, something with immediate appeal and not too much depth, something with an aura of excitement about it, above all something free enough from tradition to appeal to his undisciplined, unschooled musical faculty. The recordings of the Original Dixieland Jazz Band and later the New Orleans Rhythm Kings filled the bill to perfection.

Of Bix's progress up to and including the Wolverines episode there is no evidence of any conflict in his mind about what he was doing. The Wolverines' music was crude and naïve and, Bix apart, mediocre jazz even for the period. Even Bix is no more than promising, despite the retrospective hysteria of the Bixophiles. Jazz was a goodtime music and the Wolverines were a goodtime band. Any talk of self-expression or aesthetic morality would have meant little to its members, a collection of nondescript college boys with very questionable gifts for jazz or any other kind of music. Years later some of them confessed that Bix finally left them because the gulf between his potential and theirs had become ludicrous. The point is that while he was with the Wolverines the horizons of jazz were Bix's horizons too.

It is in the next phase of Bix's career that one can see the first signs of the dilemma which was to envelop him. The young cornetist leaves the Wolverines and eventually joins Charlie Straight's band in Chicago. But before this a most curious sequence of events occurs. In February 1925, already a professional musician of three years standing, Bix enrols at the University of Iowa, registering for English, Religion and Ethics, Music Theory, Piano Lessons and Music History. At his first interview with his freshman adviser, Bix asks to drop Religion and take more music instead, as neat a summation of his life as anybody could make. The request is refused and instead Bix is ordered to enrol immediately for Military Training, Physical Education and Freshman lectures. Four days later Bix and the University of Iowa part company forever.

The incident certainly appears comical in retrospect, but to do justice to the University of Iowa, which is more than it did to Bix, its behaviour was no more fatuous than that of most educational institutions. That a place of instruction should refuse to teach music to a brilliant natural musician like Bix, and instruct him instead in the art of cleaning a dummy rifle may look like a parody, but to Bix at the time it must have been a nasty shock. Reality is the most merciless satirist of all.

This astonishing interlude in his career is the first outward sign of what was happening to Bix the musician. A glance at the subjects he named and the additional ones he requested, reveals the process. What he was attempting to do at the University of Iowa was to revoke his own decision of years before when he refused to co-operate in the matter of his own musical education. The fiasco in the Davenport front parlour was the first crisis and the fiasco at the University of Iowa the second, and they are closely related. In some way the passion for formal knowledge and instruction, dormant since early adolescence, was awakened. The months of playing with the Wolverines were evidently months of self-revelation, months in which Bix became aware for the first time as an adult of the power of music in his life. The attempt to enrol at the University of Iowa was the first stage in the blind stumble towards orthodoxy which is the story of Beiderbecke's artistic life. The embryo-student in Bix is one of the facets of the man which fascinated Dorothy Baker when she came to write her novel about him, although the misreading of the social background and the hero's relation to music made nonsense of the whole experience, as we shall see.

The Bix legends begin to date from this time. From now on, two things impress those who talk about him, his inborn musical gift and his personal eccentricities. That master-purveyor of Bixian whimsy, Hoagy Carmichael, has claimed that his soul was so disturbed on first hearing Bix that he instantly fell off a davenport,[1] which may or may not have been intended as an oblique reference to Bix's origins.

Carmichael worked zealously on the Bix legends, from the Princeton dance dates with the Wolverines, right through to

[1] Not the most idiotic reaction to music ever recorded. 'The Ellington brass section arose and delivered such an intricate and unbelievably integrated chorus that the late Eddie Duchin, usually a poised and dignified musician, actually and literally rolled on the floor under his table in ecstasy.' *Hear Me Talkin' to Ya*. Hentoff and Shapiro.

the last days of the summer of 1931. It is difficult to know how much to take of Carmichael's anecdotage, for there is no doubt that enthusiasm for his subject and his gift for savouring a good sentimental story are apt to run away with Carmichael's tongue when Bix is being discussed. The only time I ever met Carmichael, he had half a dozen Bix stories at his fingertips, stories I had never heard before, and I confess I found myself wondering whether Carmichael had either. The catalogue of Bix's vagueness in everyday life is the conventionally unconventional one. Forgetting personal belongings, having no money in his pockets, forgetting to go to bed, leaving his instrument in a succession of bars and speakeasies. Some of these stories may have exaggerated the whimsicality of the man, but they are hardly misleading in a consideration of the musician.

Music was the only thing that had any reality for him. Iain Lang's descriptive phrase, 'a playing fool', sums up Bix perfectly. He was indeed a playing fool in the idiomatic sense of the phrase, in that to play came first, last and everywhere for him, that to play was the only function which had any true meaning, that nothing which was not directly connected with playing was worth half a thought.

Every action in Bix's life from the time he left home points to this conclusion. And yet there are men grown in years if nothing much else who glance hastily at the sums of money Bix earned and deduce as the reader of a dime magazine deduces, without wit or integrity. They make the discovery that Paul Whiteman paid Bix more than anyone else did, and that therefore Bix's joining Whiteman was a more heinous crime than his joining, say, Charlie Straight, Jean Goldkette, or even the University of Iowa. I wonder how jazz critics would react were their integrity assessed in the same way.

As early as 1922 Bix had what was for the jazz musician of the time an unusual interest in what for lack of a better phrase

31

might be termed non-jazz harmonies. One ex-student of Chicago University who worked a date with Bix around this time said that during intermissions Bix would 'park on the piano bench and improvise, much to the consternation of the other musicians, who thought he was playing nothing but a progression of discords . . . he was playing sixth, ninth and thirteenth chords which later became common in dance arrangements. In those days dance numbers were played with only the simplest harmonies.'

Victor Moore, the drummer with the Wolverines, testified that Bix attended concerts even in the Wolverine days, and of later times he says, 'In 1929, when I made my first visit to New York in four years, I met Bix downtown, and almost the first thing he said to me was, "Come on, I've got seats for the symphony tonight." After the concert we went backstage, where Bix was enthusiastically received by the musicians, who considered him a genius and were proud of his friendship.'

Moore's remark about the reaction of the legitimate musicians is intriguing and very possibly true, for by 1929, Bix, besides having become something of a connoisseur of modern classics, was beginning to evolve into a confused embryo of a composer himself, although the process was taking place despite his conscious efforts rather than because of them. Before this period, however, Bix had met a musician who was to have a profound effect upon his career and finally ended his own in either dedication or disillusion. Frank Trumbauer is unique in jazz history, for he is the only musician known to have suffered artistic death at second hand. It is as though when Bix was buried Frank Trumbauer was vicariously buried with him, for from the day of Bix's death, Trumbauer ceases to play much active part in a musical world where he had been most prominent.

Trumbauer was the diametric opposite of Bix in many

ways. As a musician, he was a minor talent although he is said, because of his drastic tonal amendments, to have become a figure of great interest and some inspiration to Lester Young. Trumbauer was an excellent executive musician by the standard of the jazz world of the late 1920s, and even more important, he was a practical man. It was Trumbauer who procured for Bix regular jobs and recording sessions from the days when they first worked together in Trumbauer's band in St Louis in 1925. From then till Bix's death Trumbauer contrived to work in the same band as Bix whenever possible. He got them both the Goldkette and the Whiteman jobs and was also partly responsible for the pattern of the great Bix recordings of the period. For these reasons he is sometimes depicted as the villain of the piece, the man who seduced Bix away from the path of virtue, the agent who handed Whiteman Bix's head on a plate. In fact, if Bix had never met Trumbauer, most of his great recordings might never have been cut at all.

The Bix-Tram recordings were the best Bix ever made, though the reason had nothing to do with Trumbauer's organizing ability. By 1927 Bix had reached the point of perfect balance between his inborn jazz gift and his artistic awareness of European music. The acquisition by an un-schooled musician of a more conventional and literate taste may eventually lead to a kind of ossification of the jazz spirit, as the career of a player like Benny Goodman testifies. But before that stage is reached when the musical limb becomes atrophied from the overtaxing of its muscles, great benefits may accrue. By 1927 Bix had reached this stage. His jazz ability had matured, and his sensibilities were now highly refined through his contact with modern classical music. Before 1926 he was far cruder. After 1928 he suffered partial and inexorably advancing paralysis because of the relentless advance of those same sensibilities. The point of balance was

33

reached in the handful of recordings he made with Trumbauer in 1927–28.

The really significant thing about Bix's solos in 'Singing the
Blues', 'I'm Coming, Virginia', and 'Way Down Yonder
in New Orleans' is that the playing is the product of a completely confident and lucid mind. The advance on the boyish
enthusiasm of the Wolverines is immeasurable. For the first
time the unbiased listener can dispense with the five ghostly
Bixes and come to grips with the reality of Beiderbecke's
greatness. Only now does the student, till now floundering in
the quicksands of the unwieldy Bix legend, find himself on
firm ground.

Like *Hamlet*, 'Singing the Blues' is full of quotations. It is
the most plagiarized and frankly imitated solo in all jazz
history. For trumpeters of the same school, like Bobby
Hackett and Jimmy McPartland, it has become a set piece, a
tiny fragment of improvisation that has come to achieve the
unexpected dignity of a formal composition.

When a musician hears Bix's solo on 'Singing the Blues',
he becomes aware after two bars that the soloist knows
exactly what he is doing and that he has an exquisite sense of
discord and resolution. He knows also that this player is
endowed with the rarest jazz gift of all, a sense of form which
lends to an improvised performance a coherence which no
amount of teaching can produce. The listening musician,
whatever his generation or his style, recognizes Bix as a
modern, modernism being not a style but an attitude. At this
point some explanation may be required, for we have arrived
at another of the apparent contradictions in Bix. If he was so
poised a musician on his great recordings, what of all the talk
of the days with Whiteman when the arrangers left blanks in
the score for Bix's solo, and the troubles Bix had reading
simple parts which his fellows could read with ease? Was Bix
illiterate or wasn't he?

Bix may not have been a very proficient sight-reader, but that does not mean he did not understand the nature of harmonic progression. Sight-reading bears the same relationship to improvising on a chord sequence as reciting doggerel does to the composition of light verse. So much for the legend of Bix's illiteracy, nurtured in a critical climate which finds incapacity of any kind romantic, and artistic shiftlessness picturesque. Whether or not Bix could read the meticulous drivel written for the Whiteman book is quite irrelevant to the issue of his literacy. Literacy in music can be achieved only by the use of the two appendages stuck on either side of the human head in rough symmetry. Bix's solo in 'Singing the Blues', with its formal logic, its subtlety, its sureness of movement from cadence to cadence, and its characteristic implication of a deep sigh in place of the extrovert passion of his coloured contemporaries, is musical literacy of the rarest kind.

The Bix solos of this period are museum pieces because they are the first peak reached by the white musician in his pursuit of what had been exclusively a coloured muse. In the person of Beiderbecke the contact of the white races with jazz blossoms for the first time into minor works of art, and naturally the character of these works is quite different from the nature of the great coloured jazz of the period. In Bix, the racial exuberance of Louis Armstrong has been distilled through an alien temperament. There is melancholy in Bix's playing, but it is not the extrovert melancholy of the blues. It is something unmistakably bitter-sweet, a quality which once led Francis Newton to draw the comparison with Watteau rather than with Bessie Smith. In Bix's day racial segregation was one of the facts of life in the jazz world, at least so far as the public was concerned. There were no mixed bands which appeared officially in public, and even mixed recording sessions still seemed an unAmerican activity.

35

Because of this phenomenon, people often see the musicians of the period in hermetically sealed compartments. There appears to be far less social contrast, for instance, between Basie and Kenton than there does between Trumbauer and Fletcher Henderson, but it is wise to remember that this segregation was not nearly so rigid outside working hours. The dependence of the knowledgeable jazzlover on recordings may tend to obscure the fact that apparently antipathetic figures like Bix and Louis played together and had a healthy mutual regard.

In November 1927, at the end of the year of 'Singing the Blues' and 'I'm Coming, Virginia,' Bix joined Paul Whiteman. The Bixophobes say he did it because he liked the sound of the salary. The Bixophiles, on the other hand, see his recruitment by Whiteman through Trumbauer as the fatal mistake which was to lead to his death, the turning point in a tragedy of Attic proportions. But in view of the way in which Bix had been reacting to music for the past five years his acceptance of the Whiteman job was a perfectly logical and artistically justifiable thing to do, keeping in mind, of course, the fact that Bix was neither a moralizing bystander nor a clear-headed adult. The casual breeze with the Wolverines had been followed by a dawning interest in classical music which led to an unsuccessful attempt to be a student. Then came the Charlie Straight Band, where some ability as a sight-reader was probably required. After that came Goldkette, where Bix met full orchestrations for the first time.

Furthermore, there were associated with the Whiteman circus two men for whom Bix in his *naïveté* had tremendous admiration, Grofé and Challis. To get into the Whiteman band appears to be lots of different things to different people. To the layman who has never known the reality of artistic activity it seems like a final artistic giving up the ghost. To the professional dance band musician with his eye on suburban respectability it seems like the crowning of a career, the procurement of the top-paying job in a financially insecure profession. To a romantic jazz fan it seems like a tragic error. True, perhaps, but to Bix Beiderbecke it seemed like the largest single step he had yet taken on the quest for knowledge, musical profundity, legitimacy, organized activity or whatever else one cares to call it. Those who can listen to the Whiteman band's dreadful travesties of musical art may find this hard to believe, but they should remember that Bix possessed neither the worldliness which twenty-five years of studying jazz has given to many of us since, nor the critical coherence to assess exactly how valuable Whiteman's music was. He knew only that there were men working for Whiteman musically literate in the conventional sense, and that to work with them must surely enrich his experience and help him towards the mystical ultimate in musical expression.

The point has been made by the carpet knights that in the Whiteman band the finest talent on earth might wither if left there long enough. If Bix had been fit enough in mind and body to continue, then would not his artistic vitality have begun to ebb? Very possibly, but although this issue may be vital to us, it meant nothing to Bix. Musicians have a disconcerting habit of doing what they want to and not what critics think they ought to do. Preserving his jazz gift was not what Bix was after. He was stalking bigger game, although stalking it with a misguided folly which appears ludicrous thirty years after.

To have warned Bix that a prolonged spell with Whiteman might have spoiled his jazz gift would have been as pointless as telling a fretting prisoner that the security of his cell is more relaxing than the chaos of the world outside. What Bix desired was some experience which would enrich him in the broad musical sense, and the fact that he was a poor enough judge of intrinsic values to think Whiteman's band could give him this experience indicts his judgment but not his motives.

So far from being a moral coward who sold out to the highest bidder, Bix was the blind unreasoning artist who followed his advancing sensibilities as only a blind unreasoning artist can, completely oblivious of the consequences. To the critics unable to appreciate the kind of musical compositions which had so fascinated Bix, this issue of his advancing sensibilities is an inconvenient fact to be pushed hastily out of court on the grounds of lack of proof. Bix was not a conveniently prolific letterwriter or diarist who chronicled his development for the edification of posterity. He was not even a conscious artist at all. Nonetheless the truth is as self-evident and as irrefutable as if he had left a signed statement. It is implicit in his movements from band to band, in the development from the Wolverines through Whiteman to his death, and above all in his later compositions for the piano.

It is the supreme irony of Bix Beiderbecke's stay with Whiteman that he came to the orchestra seeking after a state of musical grace, unwittingly endowing Whiteman as he did so with the only real musical grace that clumsy group ever possessed. Bix in the Whiteman band looking for pearls of wisdom was like Tarzan at a Keep Fit Class. To any intelligent jazz fancier the one letter Bix actually did write, the one to his mother telling how frightened he was at the thought of joining a band as renowned as Whiteman's, may seem comical enough to make even a Blesh laugh. Here is this gifted musician about to bestow on a mediocre vaudeville act his own talent, a musician so far above the jazz standards of almost all his contemporaries that today we only tolerate the horrors of Whiteman's recordings at all in the hope that here and there a Bixian fragment will redeem the mess. And here is that musician telling his mother that the Whiteman band overawes him.

The summation of the whole Bix–Whiteman paradox is contained in the Whiteman recording of 'Sweet Sue'. Every indelicacy that might conceivably be crammed into a four-minute performance is included in what the sleeve notes to the American Columbia Memorial album describe with some restraint as 'a real period piece'. Quacking brass, lumbering tubas, the tinkling of bells and the clashing of cymbals, portentous slow movements and dashing fast movements, comically bogus profundity, saccharine harmonies, teashop violins and what sounds like a deadly parody of every singer, male, female and neuter, who ever sat in the ranks of a dance-band. In the midst of this farrago, the listener may discover a single chorus by Bix Beiderbecke which momentarily dispels the nonsense as though by magic. There is no clucking inter-ference from the rest of the band. The rhythm section merely accompanies Bix for thirty-two bars, and everyone else, from Whiteman to the lowest menial on his orchestrating staff, leaves it to him.

The result is that Bix, playing casually enough, never at any time approaching the intensity of 'I'm Coming, Virginia', or 'Way Down Yonder in New Orleans', still reaches his own level of invention, and by the effortless ease of his creativity, reveals the pitiful gulf between his own mind and the minds which conceived the holocaust preceding and following the solo. It is a telling illustration of the truth that the natural jazz player will create, without even stopping to think about it, phrases which the merely literate orchestrators will never think of simply because the scope of their training and experience does not include that kind of inventive resource.

Bix's solo in 'Sweet Sue' is in no way untypical of the time, 1928. To refer to the text of this particular solo is in no way loading the dice. For a Bix solo it is commonplace enough, but it contains at least four instances of the peculiar Bixish-ness of the man's style. The phrase linking the end of the

39

first eight bars with the start of the second eight contains no rhythmic complexities of any kind, although the precision and attack with which it is played creates the illusion of rhythmic force. After climbing the chord of the major sixth, the phrase descends in the ninth bar with three notes which are archetypal for the curious elusive quality of wistfulness one finds occurring so consistently in Bix's jazz. To say that these three notes belong to this chord or that means nothing. It is in their context in the time and space of the solo, and the manner in which they are executed, that their effectiveness lies.

In the movement from the twelfth to the thirteenth bar occurs a quaver of silence in a run of quavers. The momentary break is totally unexpected because it occurs off the beat, where one's sense of rhythm has not led one to expect it, instead of on the beat, where it might have sounded ordinary enough. The result is a skipping effect which brings a gaiety of spirit giving the solo fresh impetus, and causing a subtle change of mood from the melancholia of the ninth bar.

In bars nineteen and twenty the conception of the phrasing becomes far bolder than hitherto. The time values change from quavers to minim triplets striding across the harmonies with a freedom of tonality comparatively rare in those earlier days of jazz. In bars twenty-one and twenty-two occurs a phrase which appears to be leading on from itself but which surprisingly evolves into a sequential echo of itself in the following two bars. The solo ends with rather more dependence on the fifth and tonic than is usual for Bix.

Now this kind of observation is mere quackery if it is to be used to prove that Bix had a profound mind, if for instance I were to suggest that Bix consciously played off the melancholia of the ninth bar against the jollity of the skip three bars later. When he played Bix was consciously thinking, as all jazz musicians do, no matter what the psychoanalysts may say, only of the movement of the harmonies from resolution to resolution. Whatever emotional or dramatic effects we may care to observe in the result are the product of the intuitive powers of the soloist, not his reasoning intelligence at work. But examples like this do illustrate Bix's curious individuality as a jazz musician, and his rare ability to evoke in the listener a range of emotions not so common in jazz as one might think. The very nature of the melancholia he conjures is distinctively Bixian, sensitive and reflective, quite devoid of the element of self-pity which obtrudes in so much later jazz aiming consciously at the same effects Bix produced instinctively. The 'Sweet Sue' solo is superbly musical. It has been conceived by a born musician, and that such a man could ever have seen any virtue in the feverish goings-on in the preceding and subsequent choruses, is only further proof of the mess in which the intuitive artist can land himself when he lacks the normal reasoning powers.

★ ★ ★

At the end of 1928 Bix collapsed, after a prolonged spell of heavy drinking and keeping his nose to Whiteman's commercial grindstone. Whiteman sent Bix on a cure for the drinking, and gave him a holiday with pay from the orchestra. Throughout this period of Bix's absence the band is said to have worked with his chair empty on the stand, an anecdote which may help to redress the balance of the evidence against Whiteman as the villain of the piece. Of course there was no villain. Whiteman can hardly be blamed for not pensioning Bix off with enough money to keep him in booze and seeing that he got the most salutary kind of musical experience. Whiteman was just a business man and Bix one of his employees. He did all he could reasonably be expected to do for Bix and more. He did let Bix record solos like 'Sweet Sue', even if they shattered the lunatic symmetry of his scores. He

41

paid Bix his full salary throughout an absence lasting some months. He paid for Bix's cure, and made no attempt to replace him till it was quite clear Bix was never coming back.

The fleshpot theory, having been severely battered by the story of Bix's evolving sensitivity, and broken into small pieces by the evidence of Bix's letter to his mother, finally gets ground into dust by the story of Bix's reactions to his own breakdown. The shock of being no longer able to hold his place in Whiteman's band did, to quote Hoefer, 'contribute a great deal to his poor physical and mental condition during the last years of his life'. Of course it did. The golden door was being slammed in his face, and for the rest of his life Bix seems not to have cared very much what else happened to him. But the loss to the jazz cause was largely hypothetical. The jazz world, had it but known it, had already lost Bix before he left Whiteman. And music had gained a hopeless convert.

Carmichael and Jimmy McPartland have both referred to Bix's disappointment at not rejoining Whiteman, and indeed the facts of Bix's behaviour after his first, partial recovery comprise a pathetic record. He insisted on courting Whiteman, trailing in the wake of this lumbering great orchestra, trying to persuade Whiteman and himself that everything was as it had always been.

Bix returned to the band, in February 1929, to find that Whiteman, up to his neck in commercial radio commitments, was demanding the kind of programme that even Bix knew was unworthy either as jazz or as the light programme music which had once seemed so attractive to him. In September Bix collapsed again, returning to his home in Davenport in an effort to recover himself. Throughout this convalescence, Bix thought of this mythical recovery in terms of a return to Whiteman. In April 1930 he was back in New York, looking for his job. But Whiteman no longer needed the kind of talent that Bix possessed. The Wall Street disaster had been followed by economies everywhere in the entertainment business, and jazz musicians generally found themselves hard put to earn a reasonable living.

Bix's friends, solicitous as always for the welfare of their hero, tried to persuade him to take a job with the Casa Loma Orchestra, but Bix, perhaps better educated by now as to what was music and what was an unwitting lampoon of itself, declined. Some time in September 1929 Bix made his last recordings, and in November he returned to Davenport. The three months he spent there must have produced comedy of classic proportions. Apparently Bix pottered about his home town doing a few gigs, playing at a local hotel, and so sick in body and spirit that he was barely able even to fulfil even these modest obligations. Dorothy Baker turned her back on a delicious situation when she ignored this episode in Bix's life, perhaps stranger in its way than anything else in the record.

I suspect the crowning irony must have been the sheer ignorance of the town as to who Bix Beiderbecke was anyway. The local musicians must have known and wondered. Some old acquaintances might have shaken their heads. But the real satire of the situation must have arisen from the fact that generally jazz musicians are celebrities only to each other.

In February 1931, Bix returned to New York for the last time, by now the inspiration for a full-sized legend. Throughout his absence in Davenport people had wondered what was wrong with him and how long he might be away. Rumour circulated about his sudden death, his remarkable recovery, his imminent return, his lost talent, his newfound talent. The process of deification began months before he died.

Bix remained in New York all that summer, doing some radio work, staying at home for days at a time. The story of his swift decline and death in August has many variations, and for an example of the alarming way in which his friends insisted on waxing dramatic about him at all times, there is Hoagy Carmichael's unabashed version of a day he once spent with Bix in the summer of 1931.

'I went by Bix's room one day. I met a maid in the hall. "What's the matter with that fellow anyway?" she asked. "Who is he? He hasn't been out of his room for three days." 'Tell the maid. Who is he? I looked at the maid's black face. "Just a guy," I said, and went on to his room. ' "Hi, Hoagy." Bix was lying on the bed. He looked bad, there was something missing, as if part of him were already in the dark. ' "Hi, Bix." I sat down. I was uneasy. "How's it going, fellow?"

'Bix smiled wanly. "What are you doing?" ' "Been listening to the Publisher's theme song: Its not commercial." Bix looked away and then I heard his voice. "Don't worry, boy, you're . . . ah . . . hell . . ." ' "Get your horn out. Let's doodle a little." 'He shook his head. "Ran into a girl the other day," Bix said. "She's going to fix me up in a flat out in Sunnyside." ' "Swell, get out of this dump and you'll feel better. You might eat something." 'He looked at me and the veil went from his eyes for a moment. "How's for bringing her over some night?" ' "Sure, any time," I said. 'And Bix brought the girl and came to my apartment one night. We didn't have a drink, we didn't talk music, and it soon became apparent that this girl had no idea who Bix was. And then the terrible thought struck me. I didn't know either.'

From a literary point of view Carmichael made two bad mistakes in the construction of his short story. A best friend doesn't ask a languishing hero to play the trumpet at a time

44

like that. The introduction of a symbolically mysterious woman who, like the population of Davenport, had no idea who Bix was, is an excellent box-office ending ruined by Carmichael's maddening last sentence.

It would be too much to hope that the incidental circumstances of Bix's death would be clearly defined for posterity. In fact the stories contradict each other so violently that to accept them all would be to conclude that each of the six Beiderbeckes the student comes to know, all died separate and independent deaths. For many years the stock story was the one about the Princeton dance date. Bix had a chill but went through with the gig because the promoter insisted on the condition that no Bix, no gig. But then, quite recently, it occurred to one of Bix's biographers that Princeton didn't run college dances in the middle of August. The story Carmichael once told me involved a visit to the bank, and sounded at least as credible as all the other tales.

But what is more important than the actual manner in which Bix died is the way he behaved when he sensed he was about to die. And here most of the witnesses corroborate each other. The one thing Bix took any real interest in over the last months was his piano-writing. For years he had been pottering with some half-defined compositions which he had never written down and, indeed, never really finished. The pieces were well-known to his intimates, and the most famous of all, 'In a Mist', he had recorded as far back as September 1927.

The general impression seems to have been that Bix was anxious to leave these miniatures behind him in some permanent form, and with this end in view he recruited the help of Whiteman's arranger, Buddy Challis. 'In a Mist' itself epitomizes the extraordinary conflict which raged inside the man. It is a bewildering amalgam of barrelhouse thumping and Debussyian subtleties which illustrates more pointedly than any facts or any anecdotes how the sensibilities of a jazz musician were stimulated by the impact of modern impressionist music. That is why Bix's piano pieces have remained for more than thirty years what they were when he first conceived them, curiosities. No other jazz musician underwent Bix's musical evolution in quite the same way or under quite the same conditions, and the piano pieces are essentially a product of these factors in Bix's life.

'In a Mist', 'Candlelight', 'In the Dark', are the most valuable clues we have as to what Bix would have done had he lived on into the era of the commercial big bands, or, more important, what he might have become had the campaign in the Davenport front parlour succeeded, had Bix never heard the Original Dixieland Jazz Band or the New Orleans Rhythm Kings. It seems at least possible that he would have emerged as a minor composer of some distinction, perhaps a creator of unconsidered trifles, but at least trifles conceived and written with a true musical faculty. The more one considers this possibility, and the more one remembers that for all his unqualified success in the jazz world, Bix gravitated despite himself back to the world of formal sound, the more one is tempted to the hair-raising conclusion that he only became a jazz musician at all because of the unique circumstances of his life and background. Fortunately for the art of jazz, Bix happened to have an instinctive appreciation of the spirit of the music. It was this sympathetic understanding of an unschooled idiom, combined with his genuine musical endowments, which created the classic fragments bequeathed to us on gramophone records.

Now there are the bare bones of the story of Bix Beiderbecke, and their implications are patently obvious to all those not determined to transmute every episode of artistic activity into *grand guignol* pastiche. A natural musician with a middle-class background becomes declassé through his inability to ignore his own powers. He drifts into an artistic cul-de-sac, drinks too much and dies still attempting to educate himself in the subtleties of a music which make the subtleties of his own sound gauche in the extreme. As a vehicle for fiction nothing more stimulating could be wished for. But what, in fact, did happen when the inevitable attempt was made to transmute Bix into fiction?

Dorothy Baker is the least bad novelist who ever attempted to fictionalize the jazz life, and her *Young Man With a Horn*, the least bad jazz novel so far written. Once that has been acknowledged, there remains little to say of *Young Man With a Horn* which is not violently critical. In the edition of the novel which I first read, though not in later editions I possessed, there were printed on the introductory page the words, 'A novel based on the music but not the life of Bix Beiderbecke'. This remarkable statement prepared me for the worst, and I was not disappointed. It became instantly apparent that the mind which conceived the novel knew nothing of any real significance about its hero. Bix's life and Bix's music were one and the same thing, no more divisible than Candide's disfigurements and the philosophy those disfigurements inspired.

Here the novelist was presented with a ready-made theme of overwhelming poignancy and dramatic power. An un-schooled man caught up in a tremendous aesthetic experience his training and experience have left him woefully ill-equipped to control, a man who stumbles into a new kind of artistic activity and imposes upon it an influence as alien to it as his own social and racial background, a man whose sensi-bilities have outstripped his temperament so completely that in the final reckoning the man suffers complete physical and artistic collapse. Above all, a man whose life is utterly without interest the moment it is divorced from his music.

But this evidently was too awkward a theme for Miss Baker

47

to handle, or perhaps even to notice at all. What did she give us instead? A twaddling tale of a musician with a gift 'equal to, say—oh, Bach's', who is unhappy in love and dies of dissipation. Bix was obviously the greatest white jazz musician Miss Baker had heard about, so she grafted on to him the hack figure of the artistic genius who is romantically frustrated.

That was not all. Worse was to come, much worse. Miss Baker understood as little of the nature of Bix's musical talent as she did of the nature of his life and the real dramatic element in it. The romantic tragedy of his life was not contained in the kind of silly footling romance with the extraordinary Amy North whom Miss Baker dreamed up, but with the music itself.

In place of Bixian subtlety we get nonsensical talk of going for notes so high they do not exist, '. . . at least, not on a trumpet', Miss Baker belonging to that layman society which religiously believes that ability in a jazz trumpeter is related directly to how high he can blow. And worst of all, instead of the symptomatic decline after leaving Whiteman, we get a deathbed scene in an ambulance of such excruciating sentimentality that even Hoagy Carmichael would never have dared.

The extent to which Miss Baker misread the case is best illustrated by her manipulation of the sociological facts to make her hero more sympathetic to the reader. (More sympathetic than Bix Beiderbecke, if you please!) She ruthlessly demotes our hero in class, so that where Bix was the son of comfortable immigrant parents, Rick Martin is a downtrodden member of a shiftless proletariat with no parents, no home life, no help from anybody, a character to whom music is evidently a refuge from loneliness rather than an impulse too strong to resist, as it was for Bix.

There is no mention of the middle-west, no mention of the European strain in the family, so vital a factor in the history of Bix, no mention of the unsuccessful attempt to redeem a lost musical situation at Iowa University. People sometimes suggest to me that such facts are no concern of the novelist bent only on portraying a fictitious character. But in the special case of Bix Beiderbecke the facts cannot be rejected because without them there would have been no hero in the first place. Bix was a product of the middle class and so was his music. The refinement and the Europeanization were no accidents, which is why it is courting artistic disaster to take Bix's musical prowess as the inspiration for a novel, and abandon all the contributory factors. The result will be not a man but a cardboard effigy propped up with a few cliches, which is exactly what Rick Martin turns out to be. That is why Bix was a fascinating man and a beguiling artist while Rick Martin is a silly cipher who never once gives the impression of intuitive greatness which any sketch of Bix, no matter how casual, ought to give. I wonder what Bix himself would have made of Amy North with her pathological jealousy, of the comically hackneyed drummer Smoke, who pays our hero the supreme compliment of permitting him, Rick, to befriend him. And above all, which particular dirty word would Bix have uttered when he came to that high note nonsense?

What Dorothy Baker did in fact do with *Young Man With a Horn* was to consummate, once and for all, in a permanent form, all the misconception, all the vulgarity, all the spurious romanticizing, all the distortions of the figure of Bix which have been so prominent a feature of jazz journalism for the last thirty years. *Young Man With a Horn* summarizes the whole process. It is an anthology of everything crass and cheapskate ever written by an outside world which lacked the wit and the energy to come to a true understanding of his gift and his dilemma.

One can get too solicitous about Bix. He is almost too

pathetic. He was the victim of his own artistic fecklessness, and even in his best jazz performances a victim of the irony of the jazz musician's predicament, which is that he is uncompromisingly individualistic and yet chained by the sheer mechanics of his art to the limitations of whoever he is obliged to play with. Perhaps that is why my favourite among all the Bix stories I ever read suggests that perhaps his ordeal was not quite so painful all of the time as writers like Miss Baker would have us believe. The sheer detachment of the man seems at times to be enviable. The bandleader Russ Morgan tells this story. 'I remember one time three of us went out to play golf early in the morning and we came across Bix asleep under a tree. The night before he had decided to play some twilight golf and had lost all his golf balls. So he just laid down and went to sleep. We woke him up and he finished the course with us.'

3

BENNY GOODMAN

'. . . Money is indeed the most important thing in the world; and all sound and successful personal and national morality should have this fact for its basis. . . .'

BERNARD SHAW

ONE day while talking about jazz to some students at the London School of Economics, I met a very earnest young woman who told me of her determination to compose a thesis involving jazz. Her chief difficulty was that she had no theme, and so after a brief conversation I suggested she compose a psychological history of the music. She was scandalized.

'You speak,' she reproached me, 'as though jazz were a person as well as an art. How can you possibly analyse an abstraction as though it were flesh and blood?'

And when I explained to her about the guilt complex which runs like a scarlet thread through the weave of jazz history, she seemed genuinely surprised. It had never occurred to her that a creative activity can have its complexes and its repressed desires as certainly as those who practise it, and the sudden revelation that jazz was the victim of its own psychological disorders was a deep shock to her. I believe she took my suggestion as a flippant joke, and never appeared on any of the future occasions on which I was invited to talk to the School's jazz club.

51

The subconscious awareness of jazz musicians that the art they practise had its beginnings in the most disreputable surroundings is more widespread than even the musicians themselves sometimes realize. A glance beneath the surface of Bix Beiderbecke's career reveals what dilemmas and dividends may spring from the yearning for musical legitimacy, but the process becomes glorious high comedy when the musical desire is wedded to social aspiration. That jazz music of all the arts should have developed bourgeois sensibilities is one of the most comical developments in the history of twentieth-century music, although when the musical results fall on our ears we are suddenly constrained not to laugh quite as loud as we might, possibly because we are yawning so heavily.

Had that young lady only known it, the theme I suggested was rich with possibilities. She was well aware that jazz began as a do-it-yourself music which graduated to the brothels of Storyville. At the time she asked me her question she held two tickets to the Royal Festival Hall for the latest of Mr Granz's importations. Yet she saw nothing incongruous enough to impel intellectual curiosity in the juxtaposition of brothel and concert-hall. Perhaps she did grasp it but was daunted by the enormity of the task. She need not have worried, because fortunately for us all, the process may be traced quite simply in an individual as well as in the art form generally, and the individual case has the added charm of being dramatic on the personal level.

In examining the career of Benny Goodman, the most obvious fact to emerge is that the jazz musician, no less than any other creative artist, is captain of his fate only to a limited degree, and that there sometimes arrive junctures in his career when apparent irrelevancies like governmental economic policy, unemployment figures and patterns of popular education will coalesce to mould his musical style

despite himself. Benny Goodman, who so beautifully symbol-
izes the half-witted old Hollywood myth about the poor slum
boy who blows hot licks and becomes a national idol ('But,
poppa, I don't want to be a pants presser'), is an archetype
because in addition to prodigious musical talent, he was sub-
jected to a combination of economic and social circumstances
in not quite the same way as anyone else. The imbalance
between his talent and the forces which brought pressure to
bear upon that talent is so exquisite as to appear too good to
be true. The suspicion that one is reading into Goodman's
career things which are not there, is only dispelled by the
unshakeable evidence of Goodman's recorded work, the only
evidence which really matters.

Goodman's life as an influential jazz musician extended,
very roughly, from the end of the Jazz Age to the beginning of
of the New Modernism, say from 1928 to about 1943, and it
is doubtful whether in a comparable fifteen-year period, any
sphere of artistic activity has seen such bewildering, hysterical
changes. It is literally true to say that a jazzlover who heard
Bix's 'Singing the Blues', then went into a monastery, stayed
there till the death of Roosevelt, and then came out to hear
Charlie Parker's 'Anthropology' would have real difficulty
recognizing any relationship between the two recordings. The
period between the two saw jazz move from simplicity of
conception to complexity, from unselfconscious case to high
sophistication, and it is a diverting spectacle to watch Goodman moving forward hardly at all, beginning the period as an
advanced spirit and ending it as a petulant last-ditch re-
actionary, playing the same music all the time.

Not that Goodman can really be blamed for standing still
for fifteen years. Some of his outbursts against the modernists
were a little too apoplectic to merit serious consideration, but
if Goodman moved forward so little, he moved as far forward
as most of his contemporaries. It is true that jazz evolves from

one style to another, each more complex harmonically than the last, but its individual musicians cannot possibly keep up with the process, wherein lies their tragedy. This is a truth which all but the musicians themselves seem to overlook. Once a musician matures he is straddled for the rest of his life with the nuances of his formative period. That is why at the advent of modernism Benny Carter was braver than Johnny Hodges, and Hodges wiser than Carter. The fact that though an art form evolves, its practitioners may not, is one which applies particularly to Goodman because by the time Charlie Parker suddenly began extending the harmonic range of the jazz solo, Goodman had long since become a walking anthology of all the mannerisms of the previous fifteen years. Looking back at it, we can see that when we hoped years ago that perhaps Goodman's scholastic quartets, evolving slowly into the stylized sextets, were the beginning of something, we were misreading the evidence, that really Goodman was the exact opposite, the end of something, a fulfilment, a culmination, the sum total of his own past.

Now there are certain truisms about Goodman's talent which are often overlooked, hardly surprising in view of the fact that to the purist Goodman's apparent lack of professional dignity and his obsessive trick of making money, must seem like the work of the devil. But this does not alter the case of Goodman's musical endowment. First, he always had a firm grasp of the principles of hot clarinet playing. He was an intuitive jazz musician, and the red herring of his effortless technique should never be permitted to obscure the fact. He may never have lost his mind, like Rapollo, or suffered a melodramatic death, like Teschmaker, or appealed to the amateur musicologist with the crude excesses of his own style, like Johnny Dodds, but strictly musically, Goodman's was a beautiful talent. Second, he had the kind of nimble mind which can assimilate and correlate the climate of its own environment so well that in time its owner becomes symbolic of that period without necessarily having contributed anything very original towards it. Third, Goodman, once he grew to manhood, never believed that the world of music could be contained within a jazz ensemble. Fourth, he had a degree of aptitude for the mechanics of clarinet playing which only occurs a few times in each generation. And, fifth, he was both astute and lucky.

But Goodman, when he first began to make an impression on the jazz world, was still literally a boy. The technical devotion had not yet asserted itself, and his life was still virtually the jazz life. According to Goodman's own reflections, it was not till 1932 that he began to concentrate on perfecting his technique, and the reasons he gives are most revealing. He says that he realized that a musician who could read and execute any musical score would stand the best chance 'of riding out the worsening depression'. Goodman was twenty-two years old when he arrived at that conclusion, and it makes a quaint contrast with the attitude towards jazz and survival of some of his more picaresque contemporaries. The mere thought of somebody like Bix or Muggsy Spanier sitting down to work out how best to 'ride out the worsening depression' is enough to stress the fundamental difference between Goodman and all the other Chicagoans of the period. It was no accident that it was Goodman and not Pee-Wee Russell or Jack Teagarden or Eddie Condon who became a brand image and a national effigy a year or two later.

As the years passed, Goodman's technique loomed larger and larger, until by the time I became a young musician during the war, he was our trump card in all arguments concerning the illiteracy of the jazz musician. 'Look at Benny Goodman,' we would say. 'He plays Mozart, doesn't he?' the speaker never having heard anything by Mozart in his life. And of course it was true. The retort was unanswerable.

55

Goodman was a superlative musician even by the most rigorous conservatoire standards, a very convenient thing for those suffering from an inferiority complex as to the cultural bona fides of jazz music. Francis Newton has very perceptively written of generations of jazzlovers who have grown up 'to repeat the same rare crumbs of praise for jazz by classical musicians (first or second-rate) and to hail with touching gratitude the occasional recognition of jazz by the Third Programme of the B.B.C. or similar established cultural institutions'. Goodman was the most effective bribe which jazz had to offer the musical Establishment.

It was inevitable. Technique, as it begins to amass, will demand problems to solve. It will fret at the absence of constant challenge, like a medieval knight steadily running out of opponents to vanquish. It was inconceivable that Goodman, as he moved relentlessly forward to complete mastery over the clarinet keyboard, should be satisfied with 'Royal Garden Blues' and 'I Got Rhythm', which is how curiosities like 'Clarinet à la King' and 'Caprice Paganini' happened.

This progress of Goodman's towards complete technical domination was something more superficial than and quite divorced from Bix Beiderbecke's yearning to plumb the innermost depths of music. Goodman's infatuation was primarily an infatuation with the co-ordination of mind and fingers rather than the creative process itself. But before he emerged into middle-age with his dreamed-of mastery, a million dollars and a jazz spirit that had run dry, he produced some classic jazz recordings, leaving the analysts with a far simpler task than they might otherwise have inherited. Goodman is one of the most convenient figures on the jazz landscape. He is a long addition sum, neatly and impeccably worked out pat.

★ ★ ★

The mechanics of the Chicago clarinet style are rudimentary only if one defines them in the language of musical grammar. The technical function may be described in a sentence or two, and may be learned thoroughly by any competent instrumentalist. It is in its maddeningly elusive spirit that the style becomes something which few players ever really master, for the clarinet in a Chicago ensemble has to create a great deal out of practically nothing at all.

The music the Chicagoans played at the time Goodman was emerging from the status of teenage wonder to that of adult virtuoso was not as naïve as it sounded at first hearing. It was the jazz art poised between the ensemble textures of New Orleans and the subjective brilliance of the Swing Age. The ·concentration on ensemble had inevitably to be superseded one day, so soon as the individual musician had developed his technique to the point where only a solo could gratify the creative impulse. The virtuosity of a Louis Armstrong had by its very nature to shatter the classic New Orleans ensemble form that had nurtured it, bringing jazz to the stage where the individual voice became dominant over the collective conception.

With the Chicagoans, a compromise had been reached. The ensemble had by no means been dispensed with. Indeed the all-in last chorus still represented the climactic peak of the performance. But before it happened, the soloists had their say. The tunes of the day were still simple harmonically, but not so simple as they had been ten years before. The role of the clarinet was nebulous, for he had to weave contrapuntal patterns without ever being quite sure what he was weaving a counterpoint against. He knew he had to move about the harmonies, but he also knew that he had to avoid clashes with the trumpet and trombone. He had to have a nimble mind as well as nimble fingers. He had almost intuitively to arrive at the right cadence at the right moment in the right way, and always he had to pay deference to the leadership of the trumpet.

In the tense and jagged voice of Frank Teschmaker could be noted some of the better qualities as well as some of the worst of Chicago clarinet playing. There was a disturbing urgency about Teschmaker which still makes the listener wonder whether Teschmaker was enjoying himself quite as much as a jazz musician is supposed to. And Teschmaker had a curiosity about the mysteries of music. He wondered about instrumental voicings and tried to make primitive orchestrations fit into an improvised framework. But he was a little too wild, even for the turbulence of his era. His intonation was unreliable and there were times when the music seemed to be running away with him, like a dog who takes his master for a walk.

Jimmy Dorsey, who once shared a room with Goodman, and who conducted a friendly rivalry when they used the same telephone number, was ingenious rather than inspired, and there were irritating lapses in his playing which often sounded like lapses of concentration, as in that painful moment in the Bix–Trumbauer 'Singing the Blues' when the ensemble falters as for a split second it is deprived of the support of Bix's benign lead.

Of course there was Pee-Wee Russell, but Pee-Wee was an eccentric, a special case, an intuitive accident, somebody who would never really develop because the style, with its quaverings and its falterings, its uncertainties and its last-second recoveries from imminent disaster, was the man. Nobody could ever learn to play like Pee-Wee Russell without actually being Pee-Wee Russell. Even then it could be difficult.

There are two other clarinettists one often thinks of in connection with Goodman and his early days; Buster Bailey and Jimmy Noone. Bailey is said to have studied under the

58

same teacher as Goodman, but despite an apparent mutual admiration, there is all the world of difference between them. Bailey, with his even quavers and the unsyncopated nature of his whole aesthetic, is the very antithesis of the limpid flow of Goodman in his prime, and it may be said that Bailey, who always had more than enough technique to manage, never really sounded as though he was wholly convinced about jazz.

Jimmy Noone is a different case. His liquidity and poise certainly find echoes in the early Goodman, and many musicians who know the facts of the case have testified to the connection between the two players. Coleman Hawkins rightly asserts that the similarities are so marked that 'you can't miss them in Benny's playing'. It seems clear what it was about Noone that appealed to Goodman so strongly. Noone had a fluency about his jazz which made, say, a Teschmaker or a Dorsey sound clumsy. For a man with Goodman's kind of ambition, Noone's playing must have been a distinct challenge. But what later emerged as the authentic Benny Goodman style was not really as gracious and refined a jazz as Noone's. Goodman possessed more aggression. Perhaps it would be juster to say Goodman chose to use more aggression. And it is the patterns he wove which make him distinctive, patterns of literacy which separate him from Noone, Bailey, Dorsey, Dodds, every clarinettist of the day.

Benny Goodman made his first record with Ben Pollack in 1926. He was seventeen years old, and as the recordings of the period tell us, already possessed of great assurance and imagination. On the Pollack recording of 'He's the Last Word', for instance, on the third recording session of his life, Goodman is already suggesting in a vague kind of way the shape of things to come, and in 'Waiting for Katie', a few years later, there is even a hint of the later assurance of the trios.

59

Legitimate mastery still lay far ahead, and on a 1929 recording of the composition Goodman wrote in collaboration with Bud Freeman, 'After Awhile', he executes some trills clumsily enough to make the listener raise his eyebrows in surprise that even an immature Goodman could have done such a thing. In all this early work, for all its occasional *gaucherie*, the playing bears the hallmark of an unusual talent. By the time he was twenty, the conventions of the Chicago style must have seemed child's play.

When the Charleston Chasers made 'Basin Street Blues' in 1931, Goodman took two solos, one on a conventional twelve bar blues sequence, the other based on the chords of the tune itself, and the second solo reflects fairly clearly the preference for a chord sequence more complex and technically more demanding than the blues. Throughout his career, Goodman's blues lacked the content one might have expected from a player of his stature. Too often the emotional residue is reduced to nil and the entire chorus seems to consist of simulated wailings founded on a base of the flattened third and dominant seventh, the notorious 'blue notes' that George Gershwin used to react to rather as if they were his own single-handed discovery. Goodman seems to have been one of those highly literate jazzmen who feel most comfortable meeting the challenge of a chord sequence rather more specific than the blues. No wonder Charlie Parker sounded so anarchic to him fifteen years later, for Parker exemplified the intuitive genius, a figure by no means sympathetic with Goodman's method.

Before the hiatus of 1932 Goodman made several records with his one-time idol and model, Ted Lewis, whose ethics seem to have been as questionable as his musical ability. One of the prize comedy moments in jazz occurs on a recording called 'Ho Hum', because in it is implied all the contempt the professional musician can feel for the entire outside world, and his ruthlessness if he happens to be a bandleader with an instrumental vanity his personal ability is not able to assuage. Ted Lewis was one of the monstrosities of popular music, and from the outlook of a jazzlover, his clarinet playing hovers drunkenly between tragedy and comedy. Nobody with any sensibility could ever conceivably take Lewis halfway seriously. And yet inside Lewis's own head must have resided the astonishing idea that although Goodman was superior enough to him to merit a little barefaced artistic duplicity, he was not so much better that the duplicity would be detected. And so, on 'Ho Hum', while Goodman plays a solo that nobody else of the period could possibly have played, a solo which screams out Benny Goodman with every nuance, an anonymous voice, perhaps Lewis's, shouts the encouragement, 'Blow it, Ted'. Whether this kind of counterfeit was poetic justice for Lewis after the way Goodman had started his own career with an impersonation of Lewis, nobody can say, but if it was, and if it levelled the score for a while, it was only a temporary triumph for Lewis. Goodman had the last word, as usual, at Carnegie Hall of all places, as we shall see.

In 1932 Goodman came to terms with the demands of his own ambition. He started to mix economics with art. Perhaps if the Great Depression had not scared him into building up a bulwark of technique between him and the exigencies of a precarious profession, something else might have, but significantly it was the economic factor which inspired Goodman to the chase which led in the end to the acceptance of jazz as a commodity in the markets of monopoly.

In the pre-1932 recordings there is a rough edge to his playing. It is not a rough edge with a menace, nor is it the musical expression of some personal vagary of temperament, as with Pee-Wee Russell, but rather the slight croak of an accomplished musician creating a special effect. It is hardly the kind of growl which comes to dominate an entire style,

and as the years passed it became more and more incongruous, until when Goodman resorted to it in the late 1930s it
became a little embarrassing, like a middle-aged aunt
demonstrating how she used to do the Charleston. In 'Heat
Wave', recorded with Ethel Waters in 1933, the tone is
already noticeably purer. It becomes easier every year to
chart the growing influence of classical studies on what started
as a natural jazz talent. In the same year, in 'I Got a Right to
Sing the Blues', recorded with his own band, the croak and
the scholasticism begin to make strange bed-fellows.

In the famous recording of 'Dr Heckle and Mr Jibe', the
phrase Goodman plays on the last eight of the first chorus is
typical of this new instrumental command he is carving out
for himself. The presence of Jack Teagarden affords a convenient contrast. While Goodman is still noticeably evolving,
moving forward relentlessly to some mysterious ideal of perfection, Teagarden is completely poised and quite mature,
his style a perfectly formed jewel with nothing left to iron out
or smooth away. The born jazzman, in fact, to whom a
spirited improvisation is so inherent an act that a campaign
like Goodman's would seem antipathetic and quite unneces-
sary. And yet a man who would instantly appreciate the
exultation in his own fluency which Goodman shows as he
skips blithely through what must have been for the times a
tricky sequence in the middle eight.

By 1934 the world of the Chicagoans was already receding
rapidly into jazz history, but before it ceased to be representa-
tive of the advance guard, Goodman made some classic
recordings which still represent some of the best clarinet
playing achieved in that idiom. The Venuti–Lang session of
1932 was a consummation of all the striving of the previous
few years. Venuti and Lang, the Teagarden brothers and
Goodman himself were among the finest exponents of the
style. Goodman's playing on all four tracks is in a class

beyond that of any of his rivals. In later years he was to use the nimble harmonies of 'After You've Gone' as an up-tempo revelation of supreme technical command, but on the Venuti–Lang session they took the tune at half tempo, one which always brought out the richness of its harmonic movement.

Goodman's best work on the session comes in 'Someday, Sweetheart', which opens with two clarinet cadenzas, almost laughably appropriate indications of the way Goodman's mind was beginning to work in its new attitude towards instrumental mastery. The same technical display tends to mar the symmetry of Goodman's solo over the last four bars, but until then the clarinet playing contains all the virtues of the Chicago style. His entry makes an interesting contrast with the entries Lester Young was to indulge in a year or two later. Lester would often enter with a succession of crotchets placed meticulously on the beat, and the effect would be a natural statement of the rhythmic pulse of the performance. In his entry to 'Someday, Sweetheart', Goodman chooses three crotchets, but just as meticulously syncopated, so that the melodic invention that follows is given the benefit of an effective push from behind.

At first he is content to state the theme, possibly because the melody of 'Someday, Sweetheart', has a pleasant senti-mental air about it. But in the third and fourth bars comes the first evidence of Goodman's great gift of creating melody of his own, related to the written tune but superior to it. This first truly improvised phrase is a confident lyric gesture on which the solo takes wings. Its beauty is its apparent sim-plicity, a fact underlined by the flurry of double-tempo notes following. For a bar or two the soloist is thinking in terms of the implied faster tempo which became such a commonplace in jazz ten years later, although the actual harmonies he uses are chained to the diatonic conception of the period. Later, in the tenth bar, he resorts to a pattern of time values which many years later Stan Getz was to re-echo in a whole string of recordings, a pattern of repeated notes, so that each tonality is sounded twice. It is after this that the solo tends to disintegrate in the face of would-be classical runs, but for all that the performance is a brilliant and highly evocative piece of jazz romanticism, proceeding from phrase to phrase with the kind of assurance which stamps Goodman unmistakably as a great jazz musician. Most interesting of all, it is a fragment which could never have been achieved but for its executant's attention to the criteria of Klose and Lazarus.

The great days of the Chicago style, the days when the legends accumulated and the swollen reputations were won for all time, were already drawing to a close when the Venuti–Lang sides were made. Some of the best Chicago performances were recorded at a much later date. But at the time Muggsy Spanier and Bud Freeman recorded their repertoire, Chicago jazz performances had become what they have been ever since, deliberate revivals, calculated glances over the shoulder at a musical era already passé. If by 1932 the corpse was already stiffening, Goodman did more than any other musician three years later to cause an irrevocable interment.

* * *

The events of 1935 may be explained by many factors and endless permutations of those factors, but one fact that is quite indisputable is that there had to be a Benny Goodman. His name might have been any one of half a dozen of his contemporaries, Tommy Dorsey or Jack Teagarden, Jimmy Dorsey or Glenn Miller, Joe Venuti or Bud Freeman, but whoever it was, there had to be a symbolic figure, the materialization of the American Dream in the form of a

bandleader, and the fact that it happened to be Benny Goodman is the most fascinating single thing about him.

By 1935 the pattern of jazz was changing. The repeal of
Prohibition had speeded the end of the era which nurtured
the Chicagoans and their brash music. It is at least a reasonable hypothesis that jazz might then have slowly curled up
and died away. Either it would do something like that, now
it was passé as the incidental music to the manufacture of
bootleg liquor, or else it had to make the giant step and
become respectable, commercial, accepted by the bourgeoisie.
It had to find a new audience, a wider one, formed of those
who respected the letter of the law rather more closely than
any of its predecessors.

It is now, with the advent of a fresh prototype, the Famous
Bandleader, that economics and art, profit and psychology,
hot jazz and guilt motives become indivisible. Jazz was about
to take its most significant stride away from the Storyville
legend. It was about to capture the middle-class adolescent
heart. And it did so through the agency of a musician who
had, three years before, amended his practice routine to
dovetail with the national unemployment figures. Goodman
came along with his organized mind just at the time when the
United States was poised on the brink of its recovery from the
imbecilities of the Coolidge régime. At this distance of time
it seems only natural that jazz, too, should have procured for
itself a New Deal.

The large orchestra was by no means unknown to the jazz
musician. It is often overlooked that when Goodman became
the King of Swing he was not the first monarch of the realm.
Long before him Paul Whiteman had waggled a fatuous
baton in the faces of Bix and Teagarden and the rest of them.
But Whiteman's way of selling jazz to the masses was to
drain all the blood away first. Had it not been for Bix none
of Whiteman's recordings would today be worth the wax it

65

was pressed on. His was a big band, certainly, but it was more than that. It was a huge band, a vast band, a cumbersome band, a lumbering elephantine band whose leader was apparently never aware of the beautiful parody of the real thing he was creating. Besides, Whiteman was comfortably plump, reassuringly middle-aged. This was the new era of the Proletarian Ideal, and Whiteman looked too much like a stockbroker to be accepted by the New Youth. Whiteman was, in a word, passé, no less than bathtub gin and the Charleston.

There were other big bands, far better than Whiteman had ever dreamed of, but they consisted of musicians with the wrong pigmentation for national acceptance. The fact that they were always better than any orchestra Goodman ever led, that they included in their ranks musicians with whom most of Goodman's sidemen do not bear comparison, is a fact which must always be kept very firmly in the foreground of any history of the Swing Age. The Benny Goodman band was never at any time the best band in jazz. It is debatable whether it was ever one of the best three. It just happened to be the best of those that were exploitable on a national scale.

One assumes that Goodman was at the time far too shrewd an assessor of jazz quality not to have been aware of the fact, and his actions on one or two occasions seem to prove that he knew where the true inspiration lay. There is a certain admirable ruthlessness about those actions which typify Goodman's single-mindedness at the time. It must have required considerable courage to carry a coloured musician on tour with the orchestra, but once Goodman had played with Teddy Wilson there was never any doubt in his mind that Wilson would have to become part of the Goodman act. Even shrewder was the strategy he deployed when first forming his band.

Long before Goodman had ever thought of forming his

66

own orchestra, back in the Ben Pollock days, the Fletcher Henderson band had been at its zenith. It was infinitely the most skilled large unit of its day, including in its ranks some of the most brilliant jazz musicians of all time. Henderson, a moderate pianist, happened to be an outstanding orchestrator, that is if he is measured against the prevailing environment of the late 1920s. He was one of the first men to conceive the idea of using sections of instruments instead of individuals to provide a background for soloists as well as to create an integrated orchestral effect. His writing was skilled but relatively simple in phraseology. Many of his written section figures were no more than a kind of individual riff which might occur in a more casual performance, except that Henderson was able to increase their power by using three or four voices in unison, or harmonizing the rhythmic phrase he had hit upon. As for the ensemble, the ideal was to get several men playing the melody with the same expression and inflexions that a soloist might use.

The territory Henderson explored contains more beartraps than any in the world of jazz. All the orchestral ingenuity in the world cannot justify the loss of rhythmic spirit in a jazz performance. Unfortunately the temptation to create sumptuous orchestral sounds within the jazz frame almost always results in the dissipation of the jazz itself. Henderson, keeping his effects fairly simple, was one of the very few jazz musicians who committed his choruses to manuscript without stabbing them to death with the end of his pen nib. Apart from Duke Ellington, who, for a thousand obvious reasons was unavailable to Goodman, Henderson was the natural choice for anyone who desired to form a band playing orchestrations without sounding too cumbersome, like Whiteman's, or too effete, like the spineless meanderings of bands like the Casa Loma.

Henderson's band had died of natural causes in 1934, when

67

the entire personnel had handed in notice en bloc, rather than see Henderson struggling desperately to hold together an organization for which there was not enough work to exist. Goodman's decision to form a large unit so shortly after the end of the great days of the Fletcher Henderson band was one of the happiest accidents in the entire Goodman story.

One fact about Goodman and his first band which is too easily overlooked is that in the beginning the whole episode was a huge accident, not some diabolical plot. Goodman had no more idea than anyone else that a wide public existed for jazz. In the beginning the musicians he gathered about him were concerned only with playing something fresh, something they might enjoy. It just happened that in indulging this whim, Goodman was the first man to stumble on to the gold-mine destined to yield such rich profits for years to come.

The number of factors which might be reasonably listed in explanation of Goodman's frightening breakthrough at the Palomar Ballroom are endless and bafflingly varied, from the birth of Marconi to the teaming of Fred Astaire with Ginger Rogers. The truth Goodman half-discovered at the Palomar was that the entire continent was full of young people who enjoyed dancing to jazz enough to pay for the privilege. Even then the enormity of his discovery does not seem to have hit him hard enough to convince him fully. It was not till the second great day in history of his social-economic triumph (there were three altogether, the Palomar, the Paramount and Carnegie Hall) in March 1937 that it dawned upon him that the city gates were wide open and the treasury undefended.

It is impossible to say precisely when the Goodman band stopped being a select club for musicians to enjoy themselves and changed into a corporation producing a commodity for mass consumption, but the process of change was a very gradual one and only became really obvious after some years of popular triumph. Had the big band been all that came out of the Goodman Era, history might be inclined to dismiss it with an indulgent shrug of the shoulders. After all, nothing the Goodman band played ever had half the musical content of the Ellington band of the same period. Certainly the Basie band was superior to Goodman's in all departments except clarinet playing. A good case could be made out to prove the superiority of bands like those of Chick Webb and Jimmy Lunceford, and although the Goodman band recordings still possess an engaging bounce, their chief importance today is as the secondary musical result of an accidental economic process.

It is in one of Goodman's gimmicks that the true importance lies. The band-within-a-band idea has obvious attractions for the booker, the fan and the leader, all of whom believe they are getting two bands for the price of one. Indeed, in a few exceptional cases that is exactly what they are getting. Although there are instances of leaders before Goodman featuring smaller groups from time to time, nobody had actually made one of these splinter groups an added attraction to the full orchestra. It is clear today that the Benny Goodman Trio, and later the Quartet, were Goodman's artistic relief from the rigours of leading a large dance orchestra. The group-within-a-group conception was a safety-valve for musicians subjecting themselves to a more rigorous professional discipline than they had ever known before and soon found to be excruciatingly boring.

Without any question the Goodman small groups are a milestone in jazz history because they were an acknowledgment of the further advance of that instrumental virtuosity which had been gathering ever since jazz started to advance north. In Goodman jazz possessed for the first time a man with all the attributes needed for expressing this advance in popular terms. He was young enough and white enough and proletarian enough in his origins to appeal to a large enough mass of paying customers. And, vitally important, he possessed what was by now one of the most dazzling instrumental techniques in the history of jazz.

It was inevitable that Goodman in reverting to a trio, should produce some kind of paraphrase of the Chicago style on which he had been raised. No jazz musician ever learns more than one style or school of jazz effectively, no matter how determined he may be to stay modern. Goodman was one of the Chicagoans before he ever heard of Teddy Wilson or Lionel Hampton. He remained a Chicagoan throughout the great commercial triumphs of the late 1930s, and he remains one today, Mozart or no. The trios and quartets are the Chicago clarinet style reduced to its absolute bare essentials, played on one front line instrument instead of forming part of an ensemble of three. The style is partially disguised with the gloss of a technical command and sophistication of thought that would have raised the hairs on the back of Frank Teschmaker's neck. But the Trios and Quartets are products of the Chicago style for all that, and ought to be approached from that standpoint if they are to be understood fully.

The Chicago clarinettist had always to be master of what for lack of a more academically correct term, might be called intuitive counterpoint. He had been obliged to work in a harmonic frame that was not simple to the point of despair but was yet simple enough to demand real creative ingenuity from the player. The melody was something the clarinet rarely had to play. In fact his whole justification for being alive consisted in his ability to weave complementary patterns around that melody. Either he could festoon the trumpet line with engaging melodic garlands or else there was no point in his presence on the stand at all. It accidentally turned out to be the best school in the world for a musician who might one day aspire to the heights of the trios and quartets. Had Goodman been satisfied artistically with his orchestra, probably he would never have indulged in the vanity of the small groups at all. In the trio form he found at last the ideal working frame for his talent. Never before or after was his musical personality so perfectly suited to the medium in which it expressed itself. The trio needed no Fletcher Hendersons to plan the strategy. It could make the same repertoire sound different every time it was used, and it could play unadulterated jazz whenever it chose. It might play anything Goodman cared to think up. The orchestra was taking care of the Hit Parade, often actually creating it, leaving the trio free to indulge its own fancies and, what was more important, make demands on the leader's virtuosity where the full orchestra could offer little more than mere technical dexterity. The Trio was the most inspired musical thought Benny Goodman ever had.

Its formula was as simple as its instrumentation. A piano introduction, a fairly faithful statement of the theme on clarinet, a series of improvised solos and a final ride-out chorus in the true Chicagoan tradition. Now and again they might tinker with the written chord sequence, as in 'Lady Be Good', when they uprooted the theme and transplanted it in the harmonic minor. Or they might play an original, like the wittily conceived 'Opus a Half' and 'Opus Three-Quarters'. But the whole point about the Goodman small groups is that the bulk of their output adhered as strictly to the written harmonic pattern, and was markedly similar in the nature of its repertoire, as the Chicago ensembles had been a few years before. The result of this combination of circumstances was that Benny Goodman, with his jazz experience, his instrumental mastery and his nimble mind, produced a summation of the entire musical environment which had first nurtured him. In his small group recordings he pursued the Chicago style to its absolute limits, stretched existing harmonic conventions to what seemed like their ultimate, snatched for the soloist a kind of concentrated attention he had never possessed before, and suggested for the first time that deliberate stylization might have charms to compensate for the aggressive carelessness of the jazz of a few years before.

This comprehensive grasp of Goodman's of what the clarinet had been doing in jazz for the past twenty years might be said in the long run to have killed the instrument stone dead. When Modernism finally swept away the relics of the 1930s, its practitioners very soon discovered that for their purposes there was something very seriously wrong with the clarinet. This peculiar fact has never been explained very satisfactorily. Certainly the inflexibility of pitch of the notes in the lower reaches of the clarinet's register was no encouragement. It is also true that the considerable complexities of modernism in its execution reach daunting proportions when allied to the tortuous fingerings of the clarinet keyboard. There was no doubt that the instrument sounded woefully incongrous in a bebop setting.

The result has been an almost total eclipse of the instrument in modern jazz. Nobody pretends that Buddy de Franco, for all his phenomenal technique, has a tithe of the significance of a Rollins or a Miles Davis, or even of a Getz or a Sims. Leaving aside the ineptitude, shocking in its arrogance of players like Tony Scott, there remain only the Goodman imitators, a few veterans like Edmund Hall and Pee-Wee Russell, and Jimmie Hamilton, a curious case who shows the influence both of Goodman and his only serious rival in the Musical Matinee Idol Stakes during the heyday of Swing, Artie Shaw. No young musician today thinks of becoming a modern musician through the medium of the clarinet, and the reason may not altogether be one of tone or technique.

In the 1930s Goodman stamped upon the instrument he played a conception so irresistible and so absolute that it has conditioned jazz thought ever since. When people claim the clarinet is not suited to the movements of modernism, what many of them really mean is that these movements are anti-pathetic to the clarinet style which Goodman consummated and made world-wide. His success, both artistically and economically, was too overwhelming to be forgotten. The natural parry to this theoretical thrust is the one involving Louis Armstrong and Dizzy Gillespie. Nobody made his influence felt in jazz more than Louis Armstrong, and yet in time Gillespie came along to overthrow every one of the canons of style laid down in Armstrong's trumpet playing. The difference is this. Armstrong achieved his dominance on an actual, whole, independent musical instrument. Benny Goodman did not, for so far as jazz music is concerned, the clarinet is not really a separate independent instrument at all. It is a first-cousin to the saxophone, although admittedly this relationship is a reversal of the historical facts.

No musician ever becomes technically very proficient on the clarinet without also becoming a reasonable saxophonist in the process. The reason for the spectacular role of the clarinet in the early days of jazz is that its tonal properties and the range of its upper register made it the ideal upper voice in the three-man ensembles of New Orleans. A saxophone would have been drowned in a sea of strident decibels, so the clarinet was literally indispensable. As soon as the ensemble conception was discarded, as it was in time through the virtuosity of Armstrong, then the clarinet was doomed to at least partial eclipse. Before that eclipse came, Goodman synthesized the whole process so completely that the eclipse itself became more marked than ever. And because the ensemble demand has vanished with the Golden Age of the improvised ensemble, and because also of the convenience of closed pads and the suitability of its tone, most men will prefer a saxophone when the choice has to be made. For these reasons it seems most unlikely that anybody else will ever leave a body of recorded clarinet jazz to challenge the coherence and comprehensiveness of the Goodman small groups. There will be no clarinettist to play Parker to Goodman's Hodges, or Gillespie to his Armstrong. However well any future jazz clarinettist may play, we will always wonder why he didn't play a saxophone instead, especially if, like Jimmy Hamilton, he gets closer to the spirit of jazz on the heavier instrument.

When Goodman made those recordings, the rules of jazz were very clear-cut. Harmonies always resolved in a certain way, which is why the cadences of the period are so instantly recognizable. The chord of the seventh moved with a comforting inevitability on to the chord with its root an interval of a fourth away. The diminished chord was a pleasant little extravagance, a baroque gesture that apparently resolved nowhere at all in many cases, few soloists having appreciated at the time that the chord of the diminished seventh is really only the same old dominant seventh chord with a minor ninth perched on its head and its root chopped away.

There was, in fact, a classically rigid framework within which men like Goodman had to work. To the musician bred on the subtleties of Parker and his generation, the diatonic laws of Goodman's day seem merely the result of a few hours study; the naturally endowed musician might even master them with no theoretical knowledge at all, relying on the sensibilities of a refined ear to guide him home. Goodman's supreme virtue was that despite the simplicity of the harmonic rules, he always displayed a delightful ingenuity in the way he threaded the harmonies together, an ingenuity which at certain peak moments became transmuted into real inspiration.

The session with the Venuti–Lang group is one example, and in the trios and quartets he rose to the occasion time and again. All the very greatest jazz solos are wrought so artistically that the harmonic frame on which they are suspended becomes camouflaged by the continuity and the relevance of the solo both to itself and the theme which inspired it. It is this sense of form, this cloaking of the skeleton of the harmonic frame with the flesh of artistic invention which is the rarest and most significant possession of any jazz musician, and it is the reason why the greatness of a solo never at any time depends merely on the degree of modernity or reaction of its harmonic foundation.

The best of the clarinet solos with the trio and quartet stand as homilies in the art of the jazz solo. In recordings like 'S'Wonderful', the first 'After You've Gone', 'I Cried for You', 'Sweet Georgia Brown', Goodman achieved the ultimate consummation of the style he had first begun to digest in the Ben Pollock days and earlier. Many of his phrases in these small group recordings would not be out of place in a Chicago ensemble, except that now they are being executed with a confidence and urbanity that the Teschmakers and Russells had never dreamed of, and, let it be admitted, perhaps never really desired.

By now the classical influences Goodman had brought to bear on his style had merged exquisitely with his natural jazz flair. He could now play anything his mind conceived. The long succession of small group recordings is remarkable for its technical intricacy and lack of any technical blemish. The same is true, of course, of the clarinet solos with the big band, but in the smaller unit Goodman had created the open spaces in which to move, sweeping aside all the distractions of orchestration and section figures which so often stand like clumsy signposts guiding the soloist towards the obvious. In the trio it was Goodman's inventive power and musical wit against the gods.

His integration of the diminished chord in the third and fourth bars of 'S'Wonderful' into the harmonic frame of the eight-bar phrase, the reshaping of the eight bars which open the second half of 'Sweet Sue', the fire and originality of the phrase based on the dominant seventh chord occurring at the juncture in 'I Cried for You' where the lyric says 'has a turning', all these remembered fragments from twenty years of listening suggest a jazz talent of the very highest class.

Running concurrently with this long succession of recordings with his own groups, the Goodman discography reveals another, completely independent series, likely to be forgotten, at least in the text of the Goodman story, because on the face of it they are not so appealing, by which I mean they do not present the cheapskate copywriter with the same happy cliches as the rags-to-riches success of the big band, which was after all one of those rare moments in social history when reality and outrageous romance come together and touch for a while, when the facts take on the amorphous aspect of a sentimental legend whose only excuse for existing at all is the fact that it really did happen. The Goodman success was another illustration of life imitating art, that is, if the Hollywood output of the period could by any stretch of the critical imagination be regarded as art.

The recordings Goodman made with Billie Holiday and Teddy Wilson marked the moment in his career when this astonishing duality of attitude began to be noticeable. The discography now starts to list items whose juxtaposition transforms Goodman's career into slapstick of the crudest kind. The discography tells us that the big band recorded 'When a Lady Meets a Gentleman Down South' within six weeks of the date on which Goodman played on 'Pennies from Heaven' with Billie Holiday, a session on which Lester Young created a twenty-four bar solo for which the only suitable adjective is marvellous; that he recorded 'Jingle Bells' with his own band on July 1st, 1935, and 'I Wished on the Moon' with Wilson and Holiday on July 2nd, 1935; that on successive sessions he made 'After You've Gone' with the trio and 'Santa Claus Comes in the Spring' with the orchestra; that in one four-week period in 1938 he cut some reasonable sides with the orchestra, four superlative tracks with a Wilson–Holiday pick-up group, including 'He Ain't Got Rhythm' and 'I Must Have That Man'; and a quartet session which produced an outstanding interpretation of 'Tea for Two'.

The dichotomy became more marked as time went on. Indeed, once the big band had captured the mass imagination, it could not have been avoided. By the time Goodman became the undisputed King of Swing, his orchestra, his commercial potential, his economic significance, had taken control of him. There was little he could do now but sit in the driver's seat and wait for the whole clanking machinery of the Big Band Touring Age to grind to a halt, as inevitably it had to in time. But before it did Goodman had been granted all the wishes implicit in that statement of his about riding out the worsening depression of 1932.

The movement from brothel to speakeasy is presumably a social advance from the objectionable to the questionable. The movement from speakeasy to dancehall was exchanging the questionable for the almost respectable, or even staid. It was a huge jump and Goodman will always symbolize it even if he was not solely responsible for it, nor even aware what was happening when first the process gathered impetus. But Goodman was very far from finished as a social godfather yet.

Having rendered comically obsolete the old complaint

about jazz being the music of the damned, Goodman now proceeded to remove jazz a further step away from its seamy origins and actually succeeded in making it academically respectable, at least socially. He did it with another of those inspired acts which come at just the right time and are carried out in just the right way and inspire just the right reaction, another moment in the career of Goodman when the facts take on the dreamlike quality of sentimental unreality. Vaulting ambition spurred him on to unheard-of conquests. In his personal excitement he may not have noticed that as he swept forward, he did so with such compulsive energy that he dragged the whole jazz world with him.

For the hero of a Hollywood musical of the time to have turned round to his men and suggest they play in Carnegie Hall might be expected, for such a suggestion is an excess of taste so outrageous that even the Hollywood of the time would be hard put to better it. It would be a gesture so imbecilic as to defy all rational critique, being born of the wondrous idea that the venue of a concert can in some mysterious way exalt the music played inside it, and the even more bizarre one that until jazz could conquer the world of formal music, life was not worth living, all of which is neatly symbolic of the social guilt-complex of jazz which has contrived to make its relationship towards serious music precisely that of the bastard son and the heir presumptive.

For a great jazz musician to have made the suggestion in real life, and then to act on the suggestion, is one of those freaks of circumstance attributable either to masterly assessment of the cretinous nature of the moment, or pure, undiluted fluke of the most colossal proportions, far greater than the accidental conquest at the Palomar Ballroom, about which Goodman has confessed, 'We were almost too scared to play.'

But before the culminating comedy of Carnegie Hall the

second of Goodman's Three Good Things had occurred, in March 1937. This is how Goodman remembered the day:

> We had undertaken to double at the Paramount Theatre in New York in addition to playing our job at the Pennsylvania, with no expectation that we would do more than fair business. After all, our only previous theatre bookings had been something less than sensational. So when we arrived at the theatre for an early morning rehearsal before the first show and found a couple of hundred kids lined up in front of the box office at about 7 a.m., we could not help feeling that every one of our most loyal supporters in the five boroughs was already on hand.

Either Goodman has chosen to be unnecessarily melodramatic about this affair at the Paramount box-office, instinctively shaping his story in the mould of the rags-to-riches parody his own life became, or he is revealing once and for all the accidental nature of the whole big band adventure. How slowly the facts dawned, not only Goodman, but the entire profession. Despite the Palomar and despite the steady rise of the Goodman takings, even of his less talented imitators, the sheer enormity of the breakthrough jazz had made had yet to be grasped. Goodman continues:

> All through the showing of the picture, folks backstage said there were noises and whistling coming through from the house as Claudette Colbert did her stuff in 'Maid of Salem'. The theatre was completely full an hour before we were supposed to go on, and when we finally came up on the rising platform the noise sounded like Times Square on New Year's Eve. That reception topped anything we had known up to that time, and because we felt it was spontaneous and genuine, we got a tremendous kick out of it.

On that first day at the Paramount Theatre Goodman tells us that twenty-one thousand people paid to see the orchestra. The figure is worth pondering over for a moment, particularly against the economic background of jazz music at the time. Twenty-one thousand people in one day. The moment Goodman talks of when his band came slowly into view on the rising stage is one of those pregnant moments in jazz history when, for good or ill, the entire facts of life are changed and never to be quite the same again.

The extracts I quote come from a revealing little work called *The Kingdom of Swing*, written by Goodman in collaboration with Irving Kolodin, whose interpolations between chapters consist of the superficial potted history of jazz generally accepted as the truth of the matter in the 1930s. *The Kingdom of Swing* was first published in April 1939, when its author was at the very zenith of his commercial power. It was primarily one more product of the Benny Goodman Mass Production Factory, its function and status wavering uncertainly between the fringe activity of a fan club and an advertising campaign for soap flakes. It catches Goodman at the psychological moment of his complete acceptance. For that reason it is highly relevant to any appraisal of Goodman's attitude to the music he was selling at the time.

The Kingdom of Swing turns out to be the most damning condemnation of its author, for the book never at any time attempts any honesty about jazz music. It is frankly a routine pastiche stuffed between hardboard covers, dovetailing cosily with the myths of the Hollywood vulgarians. Today the book is forgotten. Indeed it was never available in Great Britain at all. At the time it was written, it seems unlikely that a little candour would have cost very much in the way of sales.

At first *The Kingdom of Swing* is no more than distressingly naïve. Its first two or three chapters may reasonably be described as the 'kid in short pants called Benny Goodman' school of jazz journalism. However, it soon dawns on the perceptive reader that not only is Goodman determined not to commit himself on any important points, but is avoiding any kind of criticism at all. This man is 'a fine sax player', the next fellow is 'a fine trumpet man', and so on. The wretched catalogue lengthens with every page. And then, in Chapter Five, entitled 'Musician's Musician', occurs a passage that passes a final verdict on the book as no book at all, but only a package of advertising copy of the crudest kind.

Goodman is talking of 'that swell horn player' Bix Beiderbecke. The year is 1931 and Bix is supposed to be on the decline. Goodman says:

> There is a story that during one number he went out cold on the stand, and I picked up his cornet and played a chorus, but I really don't remember that part of it. It seems more likely to me that the other brass man would have played the chorus, even though I can play a little cornet in a pinch.

Six lines of print that contain within them several implications Goodman intends the reader to accept. If we examine those implications a little closer, we begin to see emerging the image of the jazz musician the author is intent on presenting to the outside world.

First it is quite clear (a) that the story is apocryphal, and (b) that Goodman has no intention of denying it. 'I really don't remember that part of it', says Goodman, to which the reader might be justified in asking, 'That part of what?'. In one breath Goodman is denying he remembers the incident, yet in the next he is hinting that nonetheless things happened that night somehow related to the incident he is rejecting.

It is all very disingenuous, but compared to what follows,

as honest and naïve as the gurglings of a baby. Posing as the realist, Goodman offers us a more plausible explanation than the one in the story. 'If Bix really collapsed,' Goodman is saying, 'his chorus would have been taken over by the other trumpeter. That seems most likely to me,' adding as an afterthought, 'although it just so happens that I can play cornet, so you see. . . .'

It is not just that Goodman is refusing to squash a ridiculous myth, or even that he poses, ludicrously, as a shy young fellow almost too abashed to confess he can play more than one instrument. What is really disgraceful about the passage is its underlying imposture, its calculated attempt to support the conception of the jazz world foisted on the public by bad journalists and worse scenario writers.

The passage takes for granted that when a man collapses on the stand it is essential that the chorus he has been playing be completed on the same instrument. But Goodman has been blustering all through the chapter about pick-up groups which play jazz on casual dates. The very title of the chapter is 'Musician's Musician'. Who cares, under such circumstances, whether a chorus that is started on one instrument is finished or not on a different instrument? If Bix really had collapsed in the middle of a cornet solo and Goodman was heartless enough, fanatical enough, unbalanced enough, to have wanted to complete the chorus before all else, then he would have played out the remaining bars on his own instrument.

Let us consider just for a few mad moments what must have happened if the myth is to be swallowed whole. Bix is involved in a chorus. Suddenly he collapses. Presumably he crumples to the ground with one of those sickening thuds reserved for such occasions. Goodman, probably sitting next to him, now has very little time to work in. The chorus has begun, for that, after all, is the whole point of the tale. Bix, inconsiderate fellow that he was, did not have the good grace to collapse during someone else's chorus, he had to go and make himself awkward in the middle of his own. Very well. Bix lies prone on the stand. Goodman decides to come to the rescue, not of Bix, but of the Jazz Muse. He has, giving him all the best of it, twenty-four bars to take over and restore to the group's performance that artistic unity he evidently craves. First he has to replace the cap on his clarinet mouthpiece. He could lay the clarinet down without bothering, but in a later chapter he takes up several paragraphs to explain why a good reed is the most important thing in the universe. Let us assume he replaces the cap and puts the clarinet down in some safe place. Let us also assume Goodman's reactions are abnormally swift, that he grasps the implications of Bix's collapse within four bars, and that he gets rid of his own instrument in another four. Provided Bix played only eight bars of his chorus before collapsing, this still leaves Goodman with sixteen bars to retrieve the situation. He leaves his chair and bends over the body. Wrestling with the figure of the unconscious man, he tugs the cornet from his nerveless grasp. This might take any length of time, but assuming that Goodman, a musician's musician, has had much experience of this kind of thing, he might manage it in, say, six bars, especially if the rhythm section has been obliging enough to drag the tempo down a little. Now Goodman has to stand up, resume his position and check the instrument for any damage. The last time I was on the same stand as a trumpeter who collapsed, his instrument was buckled hopelessly in the process. Goodman puckers his lips and tries to produce a note. As he has not played much cornet, this testing would take at least another eight bars, leaving him only two bars to complete the chorus. He hastily plays a dominant-to-tonic cadence and sits down, the situation having been saved in

83

magnificent fashion and the fair name of the Goddess Jazz still unsullied, thanks to the chivalrous resource of the young lad in short pants from the Chicago ghetto, etc., etc.

Seriously, if Bix, or even Goodman, really had collapsed, then the only concern of his fellow-musicians would have been to pick him up and try to discover how serious the damage was. But Goodman will not admit this in his book, even though the conclusion is quite obvious to anyone whose brain functions reasonably well. Goodman is intent on presenting to the world this crass vision of dedicated artists caring nothing for anything or anyone but their art, of men who literally worship at the shrine and who live a life of incredible intensified romantic activity. In other words, the jazz life seen through the imbecile prism of a Hollywood musical. Many years later fate was to catch up with Benny Goodman once and for all, making a vulgar mockery, not just of a casual book to which Goodman put his name, but of his entire life's history. Those who may have felt for Goodman when this happened, would do well to remember that little passage about the collapse of Bix Beiderbecke and duly note that the monster which finally gobbled up Goodman was the same monster Goodman himself had been deliberately feeding in 'The Kingdom of Swing'.

The reader who cannot bring himself to swallow the collapsing Bix episode may be pardoned for abandoning the rest of the book completely, refusing to accept anything it says as having any relevance to what happened, either at the Palomar, the Paramount or Carnegie Hall. Musicians who deny the validity of what is written about jazz by non-playing critics are often very justified, but it is doubtful whether any hack ever did much worse than *The Kingdom of Swing*.

It might be tempting now to turn one's back on Goodman in search of some more worthy object of study. But Goodman's attitude towards the layman's world and its relationship to and understanding of jazz, superficial as it may have been, has no bearing on the music he was producing. Even if Goodman showed this lamentable tendency to subscribe to the legends of the yellow press, the exasperating truth is that when he played, he produced jazz of the highest quality. The duality is typical of Goodman, though perhaps no more freakish than the false-nose approach to which so many jazz-men have resorted in their attempts to sell the music. *The Kingdom of Swing* is a false nose transformed into a few thousand words and sold as a book. It has no bearing on the jazz itself.

The trios and quartets were the product of a natural jazz talent allied to fanatical technical ambition. Gradually the jazz talent shrank as Goodman grew older, while the technical aspirations remained undimmed. Slowly the perfect im-balance between the two was destroyed, and the official date of the abandonment of the perfect four-man formula Good-man had evolved for himself was October 2nd, 1939. On this day he made a recording which in two very different but equally vital ways heralded the end of Goodman's Golden Age. For the first time he resorted to the sextet formula, although in effect the first sextet was still just a rhythm section plus the clarinet. The second profound change was the presence in this rhythm section of a remarkable guitarist symbolic of a new younger generation whose playing now began to make Goodman's appear flabby in contrast.

Charlie Christian had virtually no recording career apart from the Goodman sides, but in his brief life he created the only music for which the Goodman sextets are likely to be remembered. Christian is the musician usually cited as the symbolic figure caught flat-footed between the old jazz and the new, a generalization which is more convenient than accurate, being one of those half-truths which tempt people to think no further after they have digested them. In his phrasing and his inflexions Christian was an archetype of the Swing Age. The riffs he concocted, of which 'Flying Home' may be taken as typical, have about them not a glimmering of a suggestion that a harmonic revolution was now imminent. Some of Christian's riffs sound so essentially children of the middle 1930s that they can strike the ear as excruciating. But they do so because of the incongruity between them and the musical content of some of the solos rising out of them. It is here that Christian's playing suggests at odd moments that the frame that has served jazz for so long may soon be rejected as too restrictive by younger musicians.

Here and there in Christian's solos occur those same leaps, apparently quite irrational, later to be one of the most disconcerting of Charlie Parker's new tactics. The irrationality in both cases was quite imaginary, being due to the rigid conception of how a jazz phrase should move to which the jazz world was so thoroughly attuned in the 1930s. To this extent only was Christian an apocalyptic figure. Rhythmically he was as addicted as all the rest to the chug-chug-chug of the rhythm section, which is not to belittle his wonderful gift. So far from being the revolutionary, Christian was the final consummation of the diatonic approach, standing head and shoulders above almost everybody he played with. His presence in the Goodman sextet, allied to the almost comic formalism of many of the group's themes, like 'Shivers' and 'Seven Come Eleven', misled many people into the suspicion that this sextet, with its bright, ingenious little arrangements and its suave riffs, might be the beginning of a new era in jazz. Every time Christian took a solo the suspicion was strengthened because certainly there was something fresh about him. It is ironic indeed that Benny Goodman of all people, the musician who was soon to slang all the modernists, should have given Christian such lavish solo time.

86

So far from being the start of something, the Goodman Sextet was the ending of something very old. It was an attempt to bring to the small group the kind of premeditated precision of a large one. But the premeditated precision had only been created at all because the big band demanded it. The amusing thing is that for all their tailored impeccability and their tortuous commonplaces, Goodman can find for them no climaxes to match the careful stylization of the rest of the performance. Time and again Goodman returns to that Chicagoan tear-up last chorus, as though looking nostalgically over his shoulder at the good old days.

A year after its creation, the Sextet made another recording, this time dropping the vibraphone, including an extra man, and building up the front line to Goodman plus Cootie Williams and George Auld, tacit admission on Goodman's part that the possibilities of the quartet were now behind him. From time to time he did return to the smaller group formula, but always to the same themes, and always to the same kind of solo. The sextet recording of 'After You've Gone', in 1946, contains superlative technical clarinet playing, academically purer than the trio record of the same theme ten years earlier, but most of the solo is made up of formal arpeggios and scalic designs one might come across in the finger exercises of Klose or Lazarus. It was a performance different in spirit from the two earlier Goodman versions of 'After You've Gone', the early sentimental one with Venuti and Lang, and the middle-period one with the trio. It is far more sophisticated than either of the first two, and certainly more complex technically than the half-tempo track of 1932. It represents Goodman a successful man according to his own standards, for he possesses a technique so magnificent that even an exhibition like this is relaxation after the challenge of the Mozart Clarinet Concerto, a piece Goodman has recorded and performed on several public occasions.

87

The decline of Goodman's jazz reputation during the 1940s was a dignified affair, nicely paced so as to be almost unnoticed. In the commercial field Glenn Miller, one of his old colleagues from bootleg days, had taken over his crown. In the jazz world, the Dizzy Gillespie big band had put all thoughts of pieces like 'Clarinet à la King' out of the heads of connoisseurs. Goodman finally acknowledged his own artistic death when he sold the rights of his own life story. Hollywood deals only with corpses in its biographies, even if at the time of the screen version of their lives the corpses are still twitching a little. What motivates a man to sell the rights of his life to Hollywood? Money, presumably. The only other possible reason might be vanity, but then Hollywood does such dire damage to the facts and the personality that only a halfwit would be flattered by Hollywood's interest. At the time Goodman agreed to the making of 'The Benny Goodman Story' he was a reputed millionaire. He didn't need Hollywood. In holding the rights to his own life and also enough dollar bills to make him independent of the bribers, presumably he could either have refused all offers point-blank, or he could have insisted on a film which bore some relation to the truth. He did neither. He put his name to one of the most witless musical messes ever to come out of a film studio, a truth not mitigated by the fact that there was some good jazz in the film.

'The Benny Goodman Story' is *The Kingdom of Swing* made visible in Technicolor. It is the biography of an advertising copywriter's legend, not of a real life. Earlier I mentioned the phrase 'lack of professional dignity' in connection with Goodman, and I was thinking specifically of one outrageous piece of nonsense in 'The Benny Goodman Story'. Every time Goodman gazes on the face of his beloved he points his clarinet at her and doodles the melody of 'Memories of You'. I wonder whether it were possible for any great instrumentalist to countenance a stroke of deeper lunacy. The use of the clarinet voice as a way of proposing marriage fits better into the weird wonderland of *The Kingdom of Swing* than it does into the real world in which the young Goodman recorded his best work.

And yet, 'The Benny Goodman Story' is the natural culmination of a life whose main energies were devoted to sating the appetite of the masses for cheap dreams, easy to understand but very hard for any artist to swallow. It is very possible that posterity will remember Goodman as the hero of a crazy nightmare in which he picks up the body of Bix Beiderbecke and tosses it to Donna Reed, singing the lyric of 'Memories of You' at the same time, with clarinets protruding from all parts of his body, a kind of jazzed-up version of 'The Martyrdom of St Sebastian'.

Today jazz concerts are a commonplace socially as well as musically. Goodman was the begetter of these musical occasions, just as he was the begetter of orchestral fan clubs, clarinet held to the sky in profile at an angle of sixty degrees, and the legend that the Big Bandleader is a figure of heroic proportions. He started the habit of voting in popularity polls and he established the convention that when a bandleader grew big enough he ought to be invited by Hollywood to play himself in a series of musicals in which the Alice Fayes and Betty Grables of this world pursue and finally catch the John Paynes and the Don Ameches.

Above all else towers the silhouette of Carnegie Hall, the bastion of formalism and respectability that Goodman stormed and captured in a frontal assault. On that day Goodman showed his judgment of a jazz musician by including on his programme guests like Johnny Hodges and Lester Young, far superior to anybody Goodman employed in his own saxophone section. In 'Honeysuckle Rose' Young eclipses everybody else on the premises. In 'Blue Reverie', featuring Hodges on soprano, the orchestral texture makes nonsense of the normal Goodman big band processes. The curiosity of the whole evening, however, must have been Goodman's caricature of Ted Lewis in 'When My Baby Smiles at Me'. His career as a musician had started in childhood with an impersonation of Lewis. Later, Lewis had usurped Goodman's felicity on a recording in the early 1930s. Now Goodman was winning the decider by lampooning Lewis in the very stronghold of that musical outlook which could never have regarded a figure like Lewis as a musician at all. It may have been a coincidence that Goodman chose to do such a thing on such a night in such a place. Then again, it might have been his way of gaining revenge.

That is the trouble with Goodman's story, as distinct from 'The Benny Goodman Story'. At most of the crucial points, doubt is the only factor about which we can be certain. Even that remark of Goodman's about the day at the Paramount Theatre is possibly suspect. 'That reception topped anything we had known up to that time, and because we felt it was spontaneous and genuine, we got a tremendous kick out of it.' A few years ago a friend of mine who had lived in New York for several years, told me that once at a party uptown he had met a man who swore that his brother had been paid to start the dancing in the aisles. When in the course of writing this chapter I went to my friend and asked him to elucidate he denied any knowledge of having said anything about Goodman or the Paramount Theatre or anybody's brother. Possibly I imagined it, impelled by wish-fulfilment. I do not know. But with Benny Goodman, anything is possible. He may even have proposed to his wife by pointing a clarinet at her head.

4

LESTER YOUNG

*'Now we are not to consider that every new and personal beauty
in art abrogates past achievements as an Act of Parliament does
preceding ones. You are to consider these beauties, these
innovations, as additions to an existing family. How barbarous
you would seem if you were unable to bestow admiration and
affection on a fascinating child in the nursery without at once
finding yourselves compelled to rush downstairs and cut its
mother's throat and stifle its grandmother. These ladies may
still have their uses.'*

WALTER SICKERT

EVER since I first encountered it in my apprentice days, the
paradox of Lester Young has never ceased to amaze me. For
me there has been no other musical experience quite like it,
not even the disconcerting afternoon in the summer of 1947
when a clinical friend played me a record called 'Anthropology' and by so doing brought the entire superstructure of
my musical thought crashing down about my ears.

What was so singular about Lester Young? There had been
jazz musicians before him as great as he, although far fewer
than conventional criticism has allowed. His reign as a leader
of thought in the jazz world was relatively short-lived, for
within a year or two of the final parting with Basie, from
which time the gradual decline of Young's powers may be

charted, Charlie Parker was already conducting a revolution of his own. It could even be fairly claimed that Lester never dominated his field, which is where the paradox finally overwhelms. The acknowledgment of Lester's superiority over all his rivals was so belated that by the time he came to be recognized as a historically significant figure, he was already ceasing to play the kind of jazz that earned him such recognition. It is in its context of time and place that the emergence of Lester Young is so startling, for he confronts the critical mind with the problem of genuine originality only tenuously connected with anything that had gone before. Lester, it seems, owes nothing to any of his predecessors.

Jazz criticism, marred as it always has been by musical illiteracy and intellectual untidiness, has never done full justice to the figure of Young. After twenty years it has belatedly bestowed upon him its dubious accolade of adjectival verbosity, and has still to appreciate and record intelligently the importance of his presence on a musical scene with which he seems to be only distantly related.

Jazz is the reluctant art which lacks a classical tradition. Its critics, committed, by their limitations to a policy of chasing their own tails, have quite failed to establish more than the crudest canons of judgment. Most jazz critique has been based with a kind of hapless desperation on the theory of cross-influence. Henry Allen, Jnr; is said to have been 'heavily influenced' by Louis Armstrong. Ben Webster is supposed to play 'in the Hawkins tradition'. It is understood one is supposed to detect the influence of Frank Trumbauer in the tonal quality of Lee Konitz. No doubt there is a certain limited pleasure to be derived from this kind of approach. Certainly the device has proved a godsend to commentators on an art form who possess scant knowledge of its technicalities. But it is quite useless telling the student of jazz that Ben Webster plays in the Hawkins tradition unless you tell him also what the Hawkins tradition comprises. It is with its great originals that jazz criticism, technically inept and musically uneducated, has done woefully badly. Its exponents took long enough to realize that Lester Young was an original at all, for years rejecting his originality as an aberration and his artistic courage as mere perversity. Whenever confronted with true originality, the ill-equipped critic has instinctively retired in disorder, trailing his abstruse jargon behind him.

With Lester Young, whose list of idolators and imitators is now longer than that of any other man or school in the entire genealogy of jazz music, the problem is more subtly complicated, because Lester was not just original but quite isolated by the schools of action around him. It comes as no real surprise for the neophyte to discover that Hawkins recorded with Bessie Smith, or that Jimmy Dorsey played in the same jazz ensemble as Bix Beiderbecke. But it comes as a sudden unreasonable shock to be told for the first time that Lester Young actually aspired towards the Hawkins chair in the Fletcher Henderson band, and even filled it for a short time, to the evident exasperation of almost everyone involved, including Lester, or that, even more incredible, that Lester once worked with King Oliver, surely the most incongruous relationship to be found anywhere in the history of jazz. The point about Lester Young is that one is continually surprised to hear that he ever had anything to do with anybody at all.

Young represents a regenesis, a second chance as it were, for the tenor saxophone in jazz. It was all too unfortunate for his reputation that he emerged at a time when a traditional school of tenor saxophone playing was firmly established and flourishing. He was obliged to fight bitterly for some years before his revolutionary statagems acquired respectability, which is precisely why his reputation as a giant began to grow after his stature as a creative musician had begun to shrink. The story of his experiences in the Fletcher Henderson band in 1934 is one of the most ironic in jazz history, with Henderson's wife plying Lester with Coleman Hawkins records, while the saxophone section, Edgar Sampson, Russell Procope and Buster Bailey, expressed horror at what Lester was doing. As John Hammond has euphemistically put it, 'Fletcher bowed to the will of the majority, hired Chu Berry and sent Lester back to Kansas City.' Lester himself gives a subtle twist to the story when he says he asked Henderson for a release note certifying he had not been fired on the usual grounds, and then left voluntarily rather than ape the mannerisms of another. It is not difficult to picture the general scene during Lester's stay with Henderson, the first occasion on which the revolutionary came into open conflict with the Establishment.

We can excuse Henderson and his saxophonists for their reaction to Lester, for he was in effect rejecting the accepted canons of phrase-making more uncompromisingly than any other musician had before him or was to do again till Charlie Parker. In even the early Lester the very principles of saxophone playing have been drastically amended. For this reason a judgment of him is not to be arrived at merely through the possession of a recondite vocabulary and a working knowledge of the theory of matrix numbers. To an uneducated critic, Lester Young's was the most disconcerting arrival of all before the Parker–Gillespie dynasty.

Lester, being an anachronistic freak, seems to be out of context wherever he is placed. Seen against the post-Minton background, of which he is often wrongly assumed to be a part, he is a languorous misfit. Yet, considered in the context of the time when he actually did emerge, his style seems to be a startling error of fifteen years misplacement. To cast around in search of any established saxophonist who sounded even remotely like him is a futile pursuit. There are none. Even

94

among his young contemporaries there is only Dick Wilson who had some idea of what Lester was up to.

The situation was remarkable. There stood Hawkins, the acknowledged master, bestriding the era like the colossus he was, a passionate rhapsode of great romantic power. The only variations on his style were minor ones like the dry charm of Bud Freeman. And then, with no warning in the form of gradual amendment of tone or approach, takes place the most dramatic single entry in the history of jazz up to that time, the emergence of a new and already perfected style (for Lester never got very much better than that first recording of 'Lady Be Good'), a fresh style related to nothing that had gone before, mature from its conception and so revolutionary that there is literally nobody to keep it musical company. Even on some of the memorable Basie recordings of the late 1930s, involving more than one member of the *avant-garde* of the day, can be detected the occasional slight uncertainty of the rhythm section quite how to follow Lester.

Either through innate modesty or an impish sense of humour Lester himself has told how his evolving style was influenced by Frank Trumbauer and Bud Freeman. This confession would seem to be no more than a conversational device, like Hawkins' insistence that everyone is very good, or Illinois Jacquet's, that they are very bad. Trumbauer's drastic reduction of vibrato and Freeman's dilution of the customary wrath and passion of the pre-Lester saxophonists may both certainly be seen in relation to Lester's style, but these influences are merely tonal and are quite divorced from the revolution in the shaping of the aural patterns of jazz music which was aesthetically too startling a feature of the new style. Whether or not Lester was the first to amend the tenor saxophone tone, or to employ false fingerings for tonal contrast at the same pitch, or consistently to augment the chord of the dominant seventh, is not really relevant to the issue of

95

his originality. It is Lester Young's achievement that he synthesized these scattered mannerisms into a coherent and intensely personal style. The most interesting fact which does emerge from Lester's mention of Trumbauer and Freeman is that both these men were white. It seems that in Lester the process becomes apparent for the first time of the customary racial handing down of jazz being reversed. Lester represented a generation of urbanized Negroes whose attitude to life as well as jazz was profoundly different from men who had travelled afield with the music of New Orleans. In Lester the racial lines of jazz style began to get blurred over. Twenty years after 'Lady Be Good' it would no longer be possible to tell a man's colour from the tone he produced on a musical instrument. Most of the saxophonists who modelled their style on Lester happened to be white.

Before a musician can produce a tone, he must first possess some kind of mental conception of that tone. His instrument will re-echo his inner ear, and the inclinations of that inner ear will be influenced profoundly by the prevailing musical environment. There are fashions in instrumental tone in jazz, just as surely as there are fashions in any other kind of art form. The intriguing question about Lester Young is how he contrived, in a Hawkins-saturated climate, to hear the tenor in an entirely original manner, keeping in mind the fact that Trumbauer, Freeman and others may unwittingly have pointed the way. Young's own explanations for this phenomenon are whimsical but unenlightening. One feels more bewildered than ever after reading them.

The problem of whether Lester's original sound influenced the shaping of his aural patterns, or whether the originality of the patterns instinctively produced a new tone (for such an unconscious evolution is very possible), is a *pons asinorum* for the jazz theorist. There is no doubt that the two were twin facets of the same process. With Lester it is hopeless attempting to differentiate between the form and the content, or between technical cause and effect, for they are one and the same. Ever since its confrontation with the unfamiliarity of Lester's approach, criticism has tended to wriggle out of an awkward corner by tacking on to Lester the word 'cerebral', implying as it does so that Hawkins was just a country boy with his heart in the right place, or that there is more evidence of intellectual activity in Lester Young's 'Twelfth Street Rag' than there is in Coleman Hawkins' 'Body and Soul', all of which sadly begs the question.

Young's style may create the illusion of greater cerebral activity because of its sophistication in comparison with anything that had gone before. It is the obviousness of his perfect equipoise which can mislead even the perceptive listener into the delusion that Hawkins is a mere clodhopper by comparison. That equipoise was achieved by the deployment of new devices, and the delusion created by the spectral strangeness of those devices to those whose musical experience went no further afield than jazz music. The Young tone sounded more refined and his phraseology subtler. Indeed there is a sense in which Lester's approach to a chord progression is more ingenious than that of any of his predecessors. Where Hawkins would exploit every note in the chord, racing breathlessly up and down the arpeggios, Young would pass along the same harmonic path by the devious means of omission, implication and suggestion, endowing familiar progressions with a strange orientation by the use of neglected intervals, economy of notes and great pungency of wit in selecting them.

But there is nothing less cerebral about Hawkins' impeccable melodic sense in tracing a complex chord progression, the sequential beauty of his climbing phrases, or the rich romanticism of his melodic lines, which stamp him unmistakably as a creative artist of resource and culture. Where

97

Hawkins is profuse Lester is pithy, where Hawkins is passionate Lester is reflective. In such a technical connotation a word like 'cerebral' has no meaning at all and has simply been employed for critical convenience.

Now this is an issue vital to the understanding of Lester's place in the history of jazz development. Failure to arrive at this understanding means a failure to appreciate fully the fascinating innovations Lester was responsible for, and which comprise the basis of one of the most delightful, witty and original personal styles in jazz history. It was not Lester Young who brought cerebral powers to bear on a chaotic scene to produce order. Hawkins had done that years before. What Lester achieved was the creation of an alternative kind of order to the one Hawkins had offered the jazz world.

A great deal of lip-service is paid today to the Lester Young Legend, for it is understood in some vague, undefined and perhaps indefinable way that Lester Young changed the expression for good and all on the face of the goddess Jazz. If his contribution to the music is to be fully divined, it is vital that the apparent inscrutability of his genius is intelligently broken down into its component parts and correctly interpreted in relation to the contributions of, say, Goodman, Bix and Parker. Whatever we do, we have all had enough of the maundering gibberish about Les the Pres.

★ ★ ★

The Young style of the halcyon days is a highly mannered one, constantly avoiding by a hairsbreadth the pitfall of affectation. To an ear educated only by what had gone before in jazz, his playing always contained the element of surprise. The piquant deviations from conventional patterns were quite original, often anticipating amendments that became cliches in the bebop era. On many Lester solos of the middle 1930s may be detected the instinctive groping towards the chromatic progressions of descending minor sevenths which became such an overworked device in modern jazz ten or fifteen years later, although it is doubtful, from the context of those phrases, whether Lester was actually thinking in terms of minor seventh progressions at the time. His resource during this period seems to have been unlimited and he to have exulted in it so much as to have extended deliberately his own powers to the utmost. His gambit of usurping the pianist's introductory role was something quite different in character from Louis Armstrong's incredible exhibition of virtuosity in his curtain-raiser to 'West End Blues' or Benny Goodman's occasional static solo introductions with the trios and quartets of the period. In his four-bar introduction to the Wilson–Holiday 'I Can't Get Started', Lester shows a remarkable sense of harmonic mood, improvising on what seems today a commonplace harmonic sequence, but weaving what was for the times a brilliantly original melodic line subtly related to the line of the melody to come. Later in the same recording Lester improvises for sixteen bars, and it is difficult to believe that this is 1937, three years before Hawkins finally wrapped up 'Body and Soul' for posterity. In Lester's solo, passion has been replaced by deliberation, as he threads a new strange path through the intricacies of the harmonies with a dexterous evasion of the obvious sorely tempting one to the use of the most abused and overworked noun in jazz criticism—genius.

There has been much talk of that genius, most of it inept and misleading. Lester has been accorded a kind of honorary position among modernists, placed in juxtaposition to Charlie Parker for services rendered, as it were, although nobody seems to have taken very much trouble to discover exactly what those services were. They are surprisingly simple, at least in conception if not execution, and are so remote from the orbit of Parker's world that to think of these two great

99

originals as twin revolutionaries is to commit an error of aesthetic judgment of the grossest kind. Parker said once, 'I was crazy about Lester. He played so clean and beautiful. But I wasn't influenced by Lester. Our ideas ran on differently.' Lester's tonal devices are simple to the point of being glaringly obvious. Hundreds of resourceful saxophonists have since contrived to produce recognizably accurate facsimiles. Instinctively Lester distilled the tonal qualities of his instrument almost beyond recognition, to produce what misguided critics have since referred to with some *naïveté* and much shamelessness as the 'hard-reed' sound, which is something like explaining away the virtues of *Macbeth* by describing the shape of the stage at the Globe Theatre. It is not even obligatory to use a metal mouthpiece to produce Lester's tone, even though that tone in its heyday undeniably sounded metallic. But the metallic impression is an aesthetic one and has nothing to do with the material realities of Lester Young's equipment.

Having cast aside the traditions of twenty years of jazz saxophone playing, Lester actually extended the very limits of the instrument, introducing fingerings of his own that would no doubt have scandalized the late Adolph Sax. That is why Young's playing has always given the impression that its executant was intrigued by the mechanisms of his instrument more so than any of his predecessors. Unlike Hawkins, who seems to have snatched up a saxophone as a means of bridging the gulf between his ideas and the outside world, Lester seems to have lingered with an exploratory curiosity, seeking new devices. It must have required endless patience to have discovered all the alternative fingerings which formed so important a part of Lester's style. The significant point is that his technical innovations and eccentricities have an intrinsic musical value which is lacking in, say, the supersonic variations of a Ted Nash. Although Lester's playing incorporates these points technically intriguing to other saxophonists, inducing in them the question, 'How does he do it?', these devices are always rigidly subservient to the style, never being allowed to dominate and even become the style itself, as in the case of poor Illinois Jacquet.

And yet in Lester's playing, so intensely personal, so easily identifiable, there are moments when all human agency seems to have evaporated. From an executive viewpoint there seems to be not a man but a spirit behind the solos, as if Lester had tiptoed away under his porkpie hat and left the instrument to manipulate itself. No breath seems to be drawn and no embouchure to be controlling the mouthpiece. Others might occasionally close the gap between reed and mouthpiece to produce a squeak or a moment of unintended silence, but never Lester. Where the saxophone seems to have become absorbed within the massive frame of Hawkins, Lester seems to have disappeared inside his and become a diabolic extension of the keys. In the greatest work of Lester Young there is something uncanny.

The few harmonic devices Lester may be said to have introduced are interesting but, perhaps surprisingly, not particularly revolutionary. It could never be claimed that he drastically amended the harmonic structure of jazz improvisation. Lester's miracle was not the Charlie Parker miracle which brushed aside the old harmonic limitations with a flourish of impatient genius to grant the soloist so much greater freedom of movement. Lester's achievement was to accept the limitations of tradition harmonies and, remaining confined by them, nevertheless contrive to coin a new jazz vocabulary.

It is especially to the point that Lester apparently always preferred tunes which moved in the conventional cycles of resolving sevenths. His very greatness lies in the fact that restricted by these narrow boundaries he imbued commonplace structures with new and beautiful shapes sounding at times perversely complex, but which in fact bore the simplicity of true greatness. Only a man with remarkable fecundity of musical invention could have achieved what Lester did with such comparitively slender harmonic resources.

On many of his finest recorded solos he is restricted to the most limited harmonic material. On some of the Wilson–Holiday pick-up sessions, the commercial song copy was the only music visible in the studio. Sometimes the sheer inadequacy of these melodic trifles crippled lesser lights, but Lester always moved benignly along, making the most futile commercial jinkles sound poignant or exuberant. There are no apparent tricks of technique, no exhibitionism, but an unbending catholicity of taste lending grace and dignity to vehicles of the slenderest musical content. A fellow-musician once described one of these vintage solos to me in awe and perplexity as 'just notes', which is what Charlie Parker meant when he said that Lester always played so clean and beautiful.

In bars seventeen to twenty in his solo on the Wilson–Holiday recording of 'When You're Smiling'—and what more skeletal chord progression could anyone select?—Lester's choice of notes, their duration, the intervals between them and the shape he gives the whole are staggeringly original. There was at the time no other mind in the whole of jazz that would ever have dreamed of tracing such patterns at such a time. In the face of such impudent grace and felicitous execution, many efforts of Lester's disciples twenty-five years after sound hollow and bloodless, no more than a faint echo of a faint echo.

The mannerisms of the Lester Young style actually seem commonplace today, which is the most eloquent testimony of all to the fact that they have long since become a normal part of the jazz vocabulary, like Dizzy Gillespie's double-tempo runs and Charlie Parker's minor sevenths. The original thought of one generation becomes the commonplace of the next. It is the forgotten revolutionaries who are the truly successful ones.

An early mannerism of Lester Young's style, illustrated perfectly in the entrance to the tenor solo in the Basie version of 'Twelfth Street Rag', is the curiously suggestive effect of the deftly punched crotchets, soft and yet penetrative, involving the use of the tongue in a way that suggests a fine degree of relaxation and deliberation, a mental awareness of the precise musical situation, as though Lester knew perfectly well what was coming four bars later. It is this innate sense of form of Lester's that is aesthetically the most impressive quality of his playing. A transcribed solo from his great days with the Basie band, despite the eccentric aural shapes, stands as an entity, a perfect model of improvisation, balanced without being obvious, logical yet unpredictable, possessing a kind of warped symmetry of its own.

It might be suggested that Lester's solos were preconceived. Many solos familiar to jazzlovers are. If the theory of improvisation is to be adhered to unwaveringly as an essential ingredient of a jazz performance, then much of what has been passing as jazz music is not jazz music at all, but some indefinable crossbreed belonging nowhere and claiming no name. How much improvisation is there, for instance, in a Jack Teagarden performance, perhaps his ten thousandth, of 'Basin Street Blues'? How much in the entire concerted ensemble of a dixieland band playing 'Muskrat Ramble' again after playing it persistently for thirty years? How much in any recent Benny Goodman version of 'After You've Gone'. Improvisation is a red herring which has diverted the train of thought of many a jazz student, some of whom have actually disowned the entire output of arranged jazz simply because much of it is notated instead of being improvised at the moment of execution. It is not improvisation that matters to a jazz performance, but the preservation of its spirit, an entirely different thing.

I came across a most edifying illustration of this fact in 1954, when Woody Herman's Third Herd visited Europe. The bass trumpeter in the band, Cy Touff, played intelligent, spirited solos in every one of his spots. Only in more than one instance they were the same intelligent, spirited solos he played every night. In some of them there was not a jot of improvisation. Despite the soloist's projection of his own enthusiasm, his closed eyes, his arched spine, his flushed and furious face, every note he played was as preconceived as a calendar. The first time I heard him trot through his repertoire no such thing occurred to me. But the second time I watched him I happened to be standing next to Herman's bandboy leaning against the bar. He was a typical bandboy, affecting greater knowledge of jazz than half the musicians whose bags he carried, and who passed his leisure time deriding the capabilities of some of his masters in favour of Al Cohn, whose tapes and recordings he carried with him everywhere he went, guarding them jealously from all but the initiated and the worthy, pointedly playing them over and discussing them whenever one of the band's saxophonists was in earshot.

As I stood next to him he looked at me covertly like a man about to divulge a trade secret, and began humming at the same moment Cy Touff started to make his way to the microphone for a solo on 'Perdido'. I suddenly realized that the bandboy was following Touff's solo through, note for note, nuance for nuance, that he breathed with Touff, went loud and soft with Touff, sighed with Touff at the end of the chorus, and even brushed his lips with the back of his hand at the same moment Touff did. And yet it is true to say that Touff's repetitive performances were better jazz than many of

the genuinely improvised choruses of many other jazz
musicians. Improvisation is more than a virtue. It is a
responsibility demanding a degree of creative fertility which
a high percentage of respected jazz musicians simply do not
possess.

There is a common assumption among jazz fanciers that an
oft-repeated chorus requires an apologia. 'Suppose,' they say,
'a musician eventually evolves a chorus on a chord sequence
so perfect that he cannot conceivably improve upon it. What
earthly point is there changing it just to adhere to canons of
the jazz art themselves highly questionable?' Now this is a
most extraordinary defence for a practice which, as I have
indicated with reference to Cy Touff, needs no defence at all.
It is madness to demand of an artist that once he has achieved
a certain peak of creative coherence, he repeats that peak *ad
infinitum*. Was Flaubert supposed to go on writing *Madame
Bovary* for the rest of his life. Should Leonardo have turned
out annual versions of 'The Last Supper'? Occasionally a
solo which catches the fancy of its creator may indeed be
repeated *ad infinitum*, for instance Louis Armstrong's
recorded versions of 'Ain't Misbehavin' '. But 'Ain't Misbehavin' ' is only one tune in Armstrong's vast repertoire. He
evidently enjoys playing that particular chorus. But not
because he believes that in it he has reached a perfection that
cannot possibly be amended except for the worse. There are
few greater ironies for the jazz musician than the situation
wherein he is obliged to learn one of his own recorded solos,
so that the paying customers familiar with his recording can
sit there and bask in the knowledge of their own wisdom.
Flip Phillips has told of just such an episode involving the
Herman band and 'Perdido'.

It may have escaped the notice of the Play-It-Forever
brigade that the jazz musician who sincerely believes his solo
on any particular sequence cannot possibly be improved

upon, at least not by him, is at the stage in his career where he ought to retire. He ought to be concerned, not with showing us his peak but in trying to surpass it. In the process he will no doubt produce a great deal of dross, but that is one of the occupational haphazards of the man who spends his life betting on his own powers of impromptu composition. It so happens that Lester Young is not involved in any of these theories and counter-theories, for there is no doubt that he never resorted to the methods of a Touff, any more than those of a Nash or a Jacquet. The ear-witnesses of Lester in his heyday have all taken care to lay stress on the apparent inexhaustibility of his creative flow. It is perhaps truer of him than of any of his contemporaries that the limitations of the ten-inch record decimated his prowess for the listener.

Mary Lou Williams has even gone so far as to say that 'it took Lester maybe four or five choruses to warm up'. To consider this statement in the face of some of Lester's delectable four and eight-bar fragments on the recordings of the mid-1930s inspires the wildest dreams about what might have been and perhaps really was.

Here and there the evidence of the gramophone record points to what Jo Jones once described as 'the unlimited soloist' in Lester Young. The ten-inch British release of Basie's 'Louisiana' features a different Lester solo from the EP release, made available in Britain so many years later. Lester's two solos are related and yet subtly different. The shape of his melodic patterns is identical only in that it deviates sharply on both masters from the conventional thought of the time, conveniently demonstrated on the same two issues by the trumpeter, whose solo is identical on both of the masters.

In all his recorded work during this peak period, there is something refreshing about Lester's playing which is most uncharacteristic of the era. No cliches dated more swiftly than

the cliches of the Swing Age. Twenty years after, many of
them sounded like parodies of themselves. But Lester, during
the late 1930s, is not wearying to listen to today, as much jazz
of the period undeniably is. There is a certain buoyancy
which can be discerned in few of his contemporaries. Even the
urbanity of Benny Carter, possibly the most elegant player
of the period, sounds today like the urbanity of an era distinctly passé. Carter has grace, but it is the affected grace of
a time and place that no longer exist. Lester's quality is quite
different. His best work seems actually to be timeless, an
extraordinary virtue in the jazz context.

The buoyance cannot be attributed to any single element
in Lester's style, but it seems likely that one potent factor in
the preservation of Lester's freshness is the fact that he was
one of the first soloists to appreciate the value of momentary
silences, or the use of the tacit as a musical effect. Lester
stayed the flow of arpeggios of the period, making Hawkins
sound profuse, and the Bud Freeman method of stopping up
all visible gaps in the ensemble positively gauche. Economy
is one of the fundamentals of the Lester Young style. Not
even in later years, when all followed in the wake of Charlie
Parker's double-tempo exuberance, did Lester ever forsake
his stringent economy.

The most plagiarized instrumental mannerism of all, the
one most closely associated with Lester, one which has long
since become part of the jazz saxophonists' normal equipment, was the use, always with impeccable taste, of false
fingerings to obtain an effect of two, or sometimes even three
different densities of sound on the same note. It is sometimes
difficult for us to grasp the fact that Lester literally invented
these now hackneyed effects, and always used them with a
sense of form too often lacking in his imitators. The false
fingering effects were, to him, extra weapons in the soloist's
armoury, devices which could miraculously transform a

succession of notes at the same pitch, and therefore without movement, into a set of notes having little in common with each other except that the pitch itself was the same. Nine successive lower A's punched out by Lester sounded not like a tattoo with merely rhythmic significance, but a rounded, mature phrase, in which the varying densities of sound ingeniously suggested the chord changes they were to lead to.

It is when we come to examine the harmonic devices of Lester as distinct from the instrumental that we are for the moment profoundly shocked. For years it has been regarded as truism that Lester Young was a great innovator. So he was. He is understood to have been a precursor of the moderns. So he was, in a way. But for all that, his harmonic devices are not in themselves very remarkable. Probably none of them are entirely original, in the sense that many players used them before Lester. But he was the first to blend them into a personal style, making his mannerisms among the most distinctive in all jazz. The augmenting of the fifth in the dominant seventh chord, resolving on the tonic, usually at the end of a middle eight, was an effect admirably suited to the melodic whimsicality of Lester's conception, but certainly others before him had used it. Benny Goodman employed the very effect while Lester sat next to him in the same recording studio. On the Wilson–Holiday track of 'I Must Have That Man', Goodman, following Lester in the solo order, illustrates the use of the augmented chord of the dominant seventh resolving on the tonic chord as it emerges at the end of the middle eight, returning to the first theme. There is nothing bad about Goodman's phrase, but when it is compared to Lester's use of the same device, one realizes more clearly than ever how profoundly Lester changed the aural shapes of improvisation. Time and again by augmenting the fifth of the dominant seventh chord Lester imbues an otherwise stock phrase with the spice of the unexpected. Once the effect has been achieved it seems all to have been so simple that anybody might have thought of it.

In his clarinet solo on the Billie Holiday recording of 'The Very Thought of You', Lester's demonstration of the happy use of this device sounds a childishly simple affair, mocking in its casual ease and yet thrusting the short solo, whose climax it is, far beyond any other instrumental fragment on the record. Since Parker and Gillespie the augmented fifth of the dominant seventh chord, inclined somewhat towards sentimentality, has fallen from grace, forgotten in the triumphal march of the chord of the flattened ninth used in its stead, underlining once again that the Lester Young revolution was a shortlived one, harmonically at least remoter from the upheavals of the bebop age than criticism has perceived.

Lester seems also to have been the first of the jazz improvisers to have appreciated the dramatic possibilities of the use of the major sixth in the minor triad, or the chord of the minor sixth as it is known in jazz club parlance. Since Lester's zenith, the minor sixth has gone the way of the augmented dominant chord, almost totally eclipsed by its modernist cousin the minor seventh, so much more easily adapted to the chromatic movements of modern jazz. But the slight incongruity of the major sixth against the minor third in the minor triad was ideally suited to the element of uncanniness in Lester's melodic conception.

The chord of the minor sixth is, of all the discords in music, the easiest to associate with a precise emotional climate. It sounds to the lay ear somehow a little too sinister for a polite musical effect. It is no coincidence that when a motif was required for the incidental music to Barrie's supernatural romance, *Mary Rose*, it was the chord of the minor sixth that was employed to convey the effect of the ghostly shades calling the fey heroine away from earthly reality. Lester's thirty-two bar solo in the recorded minor-key trifle, 'Dickie's Dream', is a *tour de force* in the use of the minor sixth chord to evoke spectral sentiments and create melodic shapes quite new to jazz. The whole solo seems to have been conjured up by some obscure process of legerdemain.

One unfortunate result of this kind of originality was the succession of critical absurdities to which it gave rise. In an attempt to describe in terms of the layman what was musically quite simply understood, commentators sought wildly about for phrases to describe Lester's effect on them, emerging with gems like 'cerebral content' and 'abstract realism'. They were, in fact, bemused by Lester's tremendous melodic originality, and would have been most shocked had they been told that there were no new harmonic developments to speak of in his jazz.

No doubt they would have been bitterly disillusioned and withdrawn Lester in a fit of critical pique from the list of all-time greats that non-practising critics are always eagerly compiling, omitted him from their dream bands and composed punitive essays proving that Jelly Roll Morton was more resourceful and Bix Beiderbecke more advanced. It might never have occurred to them that it was in its very harmonic conventionality that the fascination of Lester Young's jazz lay. With the same meagre resources that had been at the disposal of the generation before him, Lester Young evolved a quite original and highly idiomatic style, one which boasted an independence of the familiar grooves of musical thought, enabling him to escape from the formal vocabulary of the time by the use of hitherto neglected intervals like sequential fourths and the use of the eleventh and thirteenth extensions of the dominant chord.

Now the effect of the fusing of all these diverse elements into one style was an important one not only for all jazz

saxophone playing, but for all improvisation and the interpretation of scored parts. It is difficult to imagine what a
modern big band would sound like today had there been no
Lester Young. It is even more difficult to imagine what the
current trend might be had Lester never left Kansas City or
the Fletcher Henderson episode crushed his spirit.

What would the 'Four Brothers' conception be had Stan
Getz, Zoot Sims and Al Cohn been disciples of Hawkins
instead of Young? It is self-evident that a Lester phrase
played by Hawkins would lose most of its caustic authority,
while a Hawkins rhapsodic sequence might sound very much
like a lampoon of itself played through Lester's tone. Of
course, the question of what 'Four Brothers' would have
sounded like had the saxophonists involved been Don
Byas, Lucky Thompson and Paul Gonsalves is too
rhetorically absurd to consider, for had there been no Lester
Young, 'Four Brothers' would never have been scored in the
first place. There would have been no Wardell Gray, no Stan
Getz, no Zoot Sims, no Al Cohn, certainly no Paul Quini-
chette or Allen Eager, in fact no school of modernists of
that kind as we know them. Even the tenor players of ultra-
modernism, even the Rollinses and the Coltranes, inherit a
certain ghost of a honk and a way of breaking down the
arpeggio from Lester, although of course they owe a far
larger debt of inspiration to Charlie Parker.

Lester's influence has been so profound that it is literally
impossible to chart it. His was a style more literate, more
lucid than that of any jazz musician before him, and its effect
quite different from the impact of previous great stylists in
jazz, whose influence was, with the obvious exception of Louis
Armstrong, generally confined to their own instruments.
Lester's personality permeated the entire jazz cosmology. It
was not just that he had shadows like Eager and Quin-
nichette, or even that originals like Getz and Gray owed a

great debt to him. The very methods of ensemble phrasing can be traced back to him. He has influenced thousands of whole orchestras and exerted an influence on jazz so vast and so thoroughly assimilated that today the fact that he once preached a gospel at all is inclined to be forgotten.

No matter whose company he kept, before and after, and that company is comprehensive enough to include both King Oliver and Charlie Parker, Lester Young was essentially a product of the Swing Age, the dominating melodic giant in a period unusually rich in melodic giants. The name usually quoted as symbolic of the Swing Era is Benny Goodman, but Goodman really belongs to a stage or two further back in jazz evolution, to the group of white musicians conveniently dubbed the Chicagoans. The fact that Goodman, abetted by Harry James, Ziggy Elman and a few other second-class jazz talents, once induced some high-school children to dance in the aisles of a New York theatre has tended to obscure the fact that Goodman always remained a Chicagoan, no matter what classical works he may have recorded, and no matter which modern musicians he may have employed as penance for having insulted the whole modern movement. The difference between Goodman's musical origins and Lester Young's is clearly discernible in the Wilson–Holiday pick-up sides, in which Lester is noticeably thinking in a different dimension to Goodman. In one sense the now-legendary recording of the Goodman Carnegie Hall Concert of 1938 really does have historical significance, although not for the puerilities of 'Sing Sing Sing'. The recording of 'Honeysuckle Rose' on the all-star set is a truly remarkable illustration of Lester's advance on anything existing in jazz at that time.

The background of the Swing Age coupled with Lester's inborn gifts produced in abundance one quality hitherto almost unknown in jazz. Humorists and buffoons there had always been, but the aphoristic style of Lester was something quite new. He brought the qualities of wit into the jazz context. The cultured jazzman might laugh out loud at Fats Waller, but he would smile the ghost of a knowing smile on hearing the subtleties of Lester. He is the great epigrammaticist of jazz, which is no doubt why he is more widely quoted than any other musician today, so much so that many of the innocent younger plagiarists are not aware they are quoting at all, so integral a part of the jazz vocabulary have Lester's aphorisms become.

All these facts might have been duly recognized without much confusion had it not been for the peculiar circumstances of Lester Young's recognition as an original stylist and the manner in which his musical personality asserted itself. Because of this confusion, his place in jazz history has not been as clearly defined as it might have been and ought to be. A high percentage of his admirers are either paying lip-service to a legend or privately denouncing Lester for the comparatively inferior quality of his work in the 1950s. One fact must be appreciated fully if Lester is to be placed in his rightful historical bracket, the only vantage point from which his influence may be understood. Those who talk of Lester Young really mean the young Lester. In the early 1940s, about the time when Lester and the Basie band parted company, the compact beauty of his style had already begun to decline. By the late 1940s, time and the disruptive influence of a younger generation of modernists had combined to break up the classic lines of the vintage style. The distilled purity of tone was gradually subsiding into a grosser sensuality which, ironically enough, was faintly reminiscent of the by now almost *démodé* Hawkins. Human fallibility, once so divorced from his playing, now made its belated appearance. Sometimes a low Bb disappeared completely, obliterated by the sound of hissing breath. Squeaks hovered on the rim of audibility. The sheen faded. Where once the man and the tone had seemed to merge into a purity of production never before heard in jazz saxophone playing, the sound now became a little flatulent, the fingers a shade less nimble, the mind a fraction less inventive. By 1950 the entrancing world of sound of the Basie days had quite vanished.

It was at the time of this decline that the pseudo-analysts got to work on him, critical appraisal having finally stumbled on to the truth of Lester's talent. When it was facetiously said of certain idolators that they sounded more like Lester Young than Lester Young did, there was a modicum of ironic truth in the claim, for by the time players like Eager had thoroughly assimilated all the mannerisms of Young's style—all mannerisms, that is, but not the originality—Lester himself no longer played that way. Having bequeathed his new concept to the next generation of musicians, he moved on into gentle decline. The once fulgent style had become blemished by artistic lassitude and the advancing years. When, on his 1953 visit to Britain, someone rather unkindly asked him why he no longer played 'that way', he shrugged his shoulders and quoted his age.

Ever since, Lester, a vitally significant figure on the land-scape of jazz history, has presented an embarrassing problem to those around him. Surrounded in his last days by the advocates of a far more violent revolution than his own, and spiritually at least in sympathy with them, indeed at times an active collaborator, Lester remains nonetheless irrevocably beyond the pale of the Parker–Gillespie modernism. On the JATP recording of 'After You've Gone', featuring among others Lester and Charlie Parker, the same gap of an evolutionary stage may be observed that was so evident twelve years before between Lester and Benny Goodman, only now it is Lester bringing up the artistic rear.

Strictly speaking, Lester is no modernist in the sense that Parker and Gillespie were modernists. Lester did little to corrupt the harmonic innocence of his times. The progressions he employed were basic enough for the veriest diehard dixielander to follow. The complexities of the post-war era were most antithetical to the stringency of his style, and he remained till the time of his death a kind of elder statesman, sympathetic to the spirit of change but either unable or disinclined to follow those changes himself. But if we remember once again that modernism is not a style but an attitude, there is a sense in which Lester is the most modern of musicians, having wrought changes so profound that many people today fail to realize that things were ever very different, or that Lester was once maligned for attempting to establish heretical devices which have long since become accepted principles. Self-appointed judges, intimidated by the daunting enormity of Lester's retrospective reputation as a master, have therefore been unable to believe their ears or trust their judgment on hearing Lester in the last years. 'Is this the man,' they ask, 'who is supposed to have revolutionized jazz saxophone playing? Is this the man whom every other great saxophonist mentions in his short list?' and they retire nervously to reconcile their own conclusions with the reputation they have heard about.

The explanation is simple. Recognition of originality in jazz sometimes takes a long time. In Lester's case the critics were only about fifteen years too late, not bad at all for the critics. When they did finally wake up they showered all the adjectives over him and brought him the acclaim he deserved. Only by now he was an older man no longer distinguished for the quicksilver felicities of his technique. Sometimes when I suggest that the later Lester was inferior to the earlier Lester I am misconstrued. I am accused of being a Lesterphobe. I am told I do not understand the beauty of what

Lester was doing, and that I seek for perversity for its own sake, just as people used to say Lester was doing in the 1930s. If anything I am a Lesterphile, not a Lesterphobe. And when I talk of decline I do not mean that a once great player was reduced by the years to gibbering incoherence. Lester always remained a fine saxophonist, as Benny Goodman might have said. The style of the later years was just as original as that of the Basie days. It too had its felicities and its beauties. But the difference was that by now it was no longer the most adventurous or the most exciting saxophone playing to be heard. And its motif was no longer bland virtuosity but weary sentiment. It was eminently listenable but it was already a backwater now. The difficulty is that in order to recapture the thrill of the first discovery of Lester the student has to have a sense of the historic about jazz, by which I mean he must have an adjustable ear. He must be able to sit down before his turntable and wear his 1936 ears.

When a man is a revolutionary the implication is that he is attempting to overthrow a *status quo*. The feel of the era in which Lester sprang up can easily be acquired by a study of Hawkins, the Goodman Quartet, Benny Carter and the Hodges small groups. Then, and only then, does the sublimity of 'Twelfth Street Rag', the first 'Lester Leaps In' and 'Taxi War Dance' become clear. The first recording Lester ever made was 'Lady Be Good', in 1936. A comparison between that recording and, say, Goodman's 'Avalon' or Hawkins' 'Crazy Rhythm' reveals how fresh and daring the early Lester could be.

Just as surely, the Lester recordings with King Cole and Buddy Rich some years later reveal a gradual slowing down of the creative pace. From then on, the decline is gradual but unmistakable, until with the reunion with Teddy Wilson in 1956, Lester is revealed as a tired man whose vocabulary has shrunk in inverse proportion to his gathering deification. It is

116

natural enough for people to assume that a musician's
prowess is at its peak at the moment when his reputation
stands at its highest, because the time-lag in the workings of
the cumbersome machinery of recognition is not a factor that
automatically occurs to mind. In Britain to this very day, the
recordings of the era of the LP are usually taken to be those
that show the best Lester Young. Even in the Memorial
Volumes issued by Philips after Lester's death, there is a
track or two included where Lester does not take any solo at
all, the compilers having confused him with Buddy Tate, an
error so alarming that it suggests that even those who
sincerely attempt to revive his vintage work cannot really
recognize it when they see it. It is rather as though a student
of Edwardian literature were to avow a deep respect for the
novels of H. G. Wells without ever having read *Kipps* or
The History of Mr Polly.

That is the paradox. A great musician is revered for music
that is rather less than great. It takes his best music twenty
years to win intelligent acclaim, by which time all the praises
are lavished on later work that is very good without being
epochal. By 1950 or 1960, the ear of the jazzlover had already
been corrupted by the innovations of the bebop revolution,
so that even the most thrilling originality of Lester stood in
danger of sounding old hat. After all, Zoot Sims, Al Cohn,
Stan Getz and the rest of them did it all with rather more
panache, if rather less originality, so why get excited about
Lester? The answer is that no musician can be fairly judged
and fully appreciated without careful consideration of the
time element. Jazz moves so fast that even a misplacement of
five years, or three or one, can disturb the balance of the
evidence. The catacoustic tone with which Lester honked his
way through the 1930s is one of the happiest sounds in jazz
history. The detachment of the aphorist can be sensed in
every phrase. The rhythmic buoyancy never flags. Above all,

117

the stream of phrases somehow shaped ever so slightly differently from anybody else's, never seems in danger of drying up. The diatonic approach to jazz is usually within the grasp of those who know nothing of the mumbo-jumbo of musical terminology, but in Lester they encountered a player who brought to bear on this diatonic conception a mind devious and subtle, so that the most mundane of progressions might emerge in strange uncanny garb. Lester was the first of the soloists to put paid to the Good-Time theory of jazz appreciation. His music was not the kind you could be bibulous about. It demanded full attention, developed sensibilities, some standard of musical intelligence. That is why musicians were so much quicker than anybody else to recognize his power. Unpalatable as the truth may be, musicians know more about the art of playing jazz than anybody else.

BILLIE HOLIDAY

'Mom and Pop were just a couple of kids when they got married.
He was eighteen, she was sixteen, and I was three.'

BILLIE HOLIDAY

BY A fluke of circumstance I came across the recordings of
Billie Holiday under conditions I suggest were unique. To the
ordinary jazz fancier songs like 'Mean To Me', 'I Can't Get
Started', 'Body and Soul' and 'More Than You Know' are
merely melodic shapes used as springboards for creative
improvisation. They are songs without words or sentiments.
Their titles are mere labels of convenience by which they may
be identified in the crowded world of musical themes,
exercises in musical abstraction whose personal character-
istics consist purely in the style of their harmonic nuances.
This is doubly true of the practising musician, whose relationship towards them is precisely that of the aspiring
sculptor towards a block of uncut stone. He is all too aware
of their texture, their shape, and the tempos their construction implies, so that when he comes across a vocal performance of them he will often find them pedestrian and even
unfamiliar.

But when I first encountered Billie Holiday's recorded
version of 'Mean To Me' I possessed none of the questionable experience of the adult round which might have debased

the currency of my critical faculties. Until I heard Billie
Holiday sing 'Mean To Me' I was unaware that the song
existed. This innocence had a curious effect. For several
years I accepted these songs in the form in which Billie
Holiday had introduced them to me. I sensed they were great
jazz performances without knowing why, although looking
back on it, I was no doubt charmed beyond all resistance by
the salty appeal of the diction, the tactful poise of the
accompaniments and above all by the exuberance of the
rhythm. The Teddy Wilson–Lester Young–Benny Goodman
pick-up groups were my first experience of art potent enough
to induce me to try my own hand. It was their virtues which
tempted me to enter the jazz world, to aspire towards the kind
of musical expression which in the end was never achieved
because it meant being as good as Lester Young.

The jazz of the Wilson–Holiday groups was obviously
related to the earlier jazz with which I was familiar, but it had
about it a quality too subtle for me to have then defined. Had
I known it, recordings like 'Laughing at Life', 'Sugar' and
'He Ain't Got Rhythm' represented a stage in jazz development when the instrumental sophistication of its soloists was
in perfect sympathy with the more adventurous harmonic
conventions of the day. The imbalance between these two
factors was more delicately poised than ever before or since
in jazz, now approaching the stage when all the possibilities
of diatonic harmony were being realized, the end product of
an evolution as natural and as inevitable as the growth of an
amoeba.

But the day I heard Billie Holiday for the first time I knew
nothing of all this. All I was aware of was the fact that this
jazz was texturally richer than any small-group jazz I had
heard before, that it had managed in some impalpable way to
ignore the impasse of the Chicagoans as though the impasse
had never existed, which of course for musicians like Young

and Wilson, Webster and Carter, it never had, and that somehow the brave piping voice of the singer lent the music an
ironic edge which seemed suddenly to bring it much closer
to external realities than it had ever seemed before. Some
years went by and I became a musician. The songs I had
learned from Billie Holiday went, lamentably, out of fashion,
apart from a few timeless pieces like 'On the Sunny Side of
the Street' and 'Pennies From Heaven'. 'I Can't Get Started'
was certainly popular in the scrambling, inchoate days of the
New Jazz, but it was the 'I Can't Get Started' of a harmonic
adventurer like Dizzy Gillespie, not the 'I Can't Get Started'
of a soloist like Lester Young, whose inner quietism came
from an instinctive understanding that his style, by the time
he recorded the tune with Billie Holiday, was now an artistic
constancy, beyond the petty considerations of acceptance and
rejection.

The jazz of the later 1940s was the direct opposite of the
pick-up music of ten years before, because it was vainly
ambitious, self-consciously revolutionary, and somehow
nervously aware that, arriving at a time when there were a
few signs that the outside world might one day sit up and
take notice, it was playing for higher stakes than any the
Chicagoans or the Swing Kings had ever dreamed of. Too
much of it was unrelaxed and therefore the direct antithesis
of what Billie Holiday had already achieved.

All of this was quite understandable. It was precisely
because of the mastery of men like Young, Wilson, Carter,
Eldridge, Hodges and the rest of the sidemen of the Wilson–
Holiday recordings that the generation succeeding them was
inspired to dump the entire legacy of the 1930s, at least for
a while, and seek the broader harmonic licence that alone
could enable them to escape from definitive solo patterns like
Hawkins' 'Body and Soul' and Lester Young's 'Twelfth
Street Rag'. It is a process repeated in all the arts periodically.

The Youngs and the Hawkinses had exhausted the form for the time being, and the only alternative to stagnation was extension of the form.

There were several unfortunate by-products of this upsurge of activity. One of them was the eclipse of the Wilson–Holiday era, its leading figures, its conventions, even its repertoire. Practically the whole of Billie Holiday's recorded output consisted of songs which were now considered by very young men to be distinctly passé. The last word in vocal profundity was considered to be 'Lover Man', a record which flattered only to deceive, for it seemed to promise the modern equivalent of Billie Holiday's vocal formula of the 1930s. On the surface the formula was indeed the same, with Parker and Gillespie playing the roles of Lester and Buck Clayton. The performance was still built around the singer. As time proved, Sarah Vaughan was soon to turn her back on this kind of jazz record, while the nearest thing to a replacement for the vintage Billie was Billie herself, now ten years older and an artist of an entirely different character, as we shall see. But when modernism first burst upon the astonished ears of a generation of jazzlovers bred on the resolving felicities of Benny Carter and Benny Goodman, the casual masterpieces of the Vocalion sessions seemed quaint in their naïveté.

Modernism slowly became part of the status quo. As the necessity for the ruthless anarchy slowly faded away, the New Jazz became absorbed into the main body of the music, as inevitably it had to be. It was no longer an outrageous joke for the new masters to borrow the material of the old ones. Miles Davis could record 'Bye, Bye, Blackbird', with a perfectly straight face, even perhaps too straight a face. Once the revolution became respectable, it could afford to become reasonable too, and acknowledge officially what its leading lights had always acknowledged privately, that there was a great deal worth salvaging from the generation it had opposed so violently.

The enlightenment permeated every stratum of jazz activity, until the inevitable happened. I was working in a sextet on one night in a London jazzclub when somebody produced an orchestration of 'Mean To Me', complete with chord symbols. It was then, twelve years after, that it dawned upon me exactly what it was Billie Holiday had been doing with such material. The tune itself now sounded like the work of a dullard, its harmonies uninspiring and its melody fraudulently sequential. I realized that when she recorded it in 1937, Billie Holiday had produced a version so rich in creative resource that it had instantly become for me the definitive edition, without my realizing that I had rejected anybody else's. 'Mean To Me', to do it justice, is really quite a charming song, skilfully constructed and reasonably helpful to a jazz musician, but it is something vastly removed from Billie Holiday's recording of the same name.

I cannot exaggerate the shock to my musical system this one harmless orchestration caused. My emotions were a confused mixture of the indescribable rapture the professional feels when his innocence, long since forgotten, is suddenly handed back to him on a plate, and genuine bewilderment that I should have ever joined in the wholesale renunciation of the 1930s my own generation seemed to think was obligatory for playing modern jazz.

From then on my enthusiasm for Billie Holiday became a rational as well as an emotional thing, for I was now able to understand with the wisdom of hindsight what I had only vaguely sensed many years before. Of course the experience with 'Mean To Me' repeated itself with many other songs in the Holiday repertoire. I had literally to learn these tunes all over again. Sometimes the wrench was too much. I never could, for instance, reorientate my thinking far enough to

accept the written line of 'I'll Get By', because Billie's version
had for too long been the true one for me, the first version of
any musical performance being the one which for obvious
reasons makes the deepest impression.

And the conclusion I eventually came to was that Billie
Holiday is one of the most significant jazz artists who ever
lived, more significant by a thousandfold than many of the
mimetic artisan craftsmen whose nuances we all strove to
acquire as fashion changed, that she was one of the most
remarkable natural musicians jazz has seen, so natural in fact
that it is very doubtful whether she was ever fully aware of it,
and that in being obliged to use words at certain pitches instead of just the pitches themselves, her unqualified artistic
triumph was all the more remarkable because it required her,
almost inadvertently, to prove the universality of jazz in a
way no instrumentalist could possibly have done.

* * *

The primary fact about the career of Billie Holiday is its
purity. This is a truth so obvious and so unconditional that it
often tends to be overlooked, or worse, taken for granted. It
is an astonishing truth when considered in the context of the
musical world in which Billie Holiday lived and worked.
For a woman to sing for nearly thirty years without once
bowing to the demands of the world of commercial music
surrounding her sounds literally impossible when we remember that most of her material was borrowed from that
very world, a world that has never regarded jazz as anything
much more than an undefended treasurehouse to be pillaged
at leisure, with vast sums of money to be made out of sickly,
bowdlerized versions.

It may, on the face of it, appear unpardonable to claim as a
virtue in the jazz art an integrity taken for granted in most
others. After all, to claim respect for a singer merely because

she refused to commit artistic suicide seems like a very negative compliment. But it must be remembered that Billie Holiday's position was unique in that she had either to borrow the songs written for the popular market or elect not to sing anything at all. Because she had to use these songs, it was remarkable that she never succumbed to the stylistic outrages to which many of them so obligingly lend themselves. Billie Holiday was chained by circumstance to the jingles of Tin Pan Alley, explaining the perception of Charles Fox's remark that while Bessie Smith drew on the poetry of the Blues, Billie Holiday had largely to create her own. It raises a vital point, this dubious material. It was the price that people like Billie Holiday had to pay for the handicap of not being household words, like Shirley Temple, Kate Smith and Rudy Vallee. The companies for which Billie Holiday recorded required some bait to catch the unenlightened eye of the record-buying public, for Billie was never issued in the Race series of recordings that followed a prescribed racial pattern. Her work was thrown into the open market, yet another musical result of a sociological phenomenon, the urbanization of the American Negro as he moved into the industrialized areas and fought for the same fruits of city life as his white counterpart. Billie was cut off from the rich poetic imagery of the blues on two counts, the lack of demand for it among the audiences on which companies like Vocalion had their eye, and her own environment. There were no cotton fields in Baltimore, but there were plenty of clubs and dance halls.

That was how Billie Holiday came to record tunes like 'If You Were Mine' and 'Me, Myself and I', which, left to the kind of performers for whom they were probably intended, would have been forgotten long ago. But Billie rose far above these limitations, making the instinctive adjustment between the triviality of the material and the grandeur of her own conception. It so happens that 'Me, Myself and I' is one of the great vocal masterpieces of jazz.

The first Billie Holiday recording sessions may be described as a false start. They typify the levity of approach that riddles jazz history in all its phases. Of the countless songs she might have sung, Billie works over one dismal little piece called 'Riffin' the Scotch', whose only virtue is its limitation to three minutes duration. Consider the situation. A young girl appears who possesses the rarest of all jazz gifts, the ability of a singer to hold her own with outstanding instrumentalists. She gets the chance to record, with musicians as distinguished as Benny Goodman and the Teagarden brothers. The result is a lyrical outrage like 'Riffin' the Scotch'. It was Goodman's tune and Goodman's invitation to record, but it is depressing to think that the same man who could appreciate Billie's gifts well enough to ask her to the studio should then saddle her with some inane concoction of his own. Another instance of Goodman looking for the main chance, another phase in the campaign to 'ride out the worsening depression'.

The session is interesting in another way, for it was the only time Billie ever got mixed up with the older generation in a recording studio. Not that Goodman or the Teagarden brothers were old men, but they favoured a style that was already in the process of being superseded. Billie was essentially a child of the Swing Age, a purveyor of art music rather than the folk poetry of Bessie Smith. Her aura was essentially that of witty stylists like Teddy Wilson. In 'Riffin' the Scotch', the accompanying group represents the tail-end of a dying era rather than the early flourishes on an emergent one. The jolly extroversion of the whole accompaniment made quite the wrong setting. Jazz was passing out of the brash stage. Billie required the poise of a group more sophisticated than a Chicago ensemble with a few scored passages thrown in. It is a depressing reminder of the realities of the jazz life that the greatest singer of her generation should make her recording début with a cheapjack lyric whose final cadence is the excruciating jocosity of a cork being pulled out of a bottle.

This episode occurred in December 1933, and it was not for another eighteen months that the first masterpieces began to appear. In the summer of 1935 she recorded four sides much closer in spirit to the work she was to produce over the next ten years. Indeed these tracks are already typical of the vintage Billie Holiday. Not all of them were pitched in quite the same stylistic key, because one of them was virtually by the Benny Goodman Trio with a few extras thrown in. 'Miss Brown To You' opens with brilliant interplay between Goodman and Teddy Wilson, typical of the small-group series beginning to appear about this time. The rest of the session was rather different and established a pattern for all the successful Holiday recordings of the next few years. 'What a Little Moonlight Can Do' and 'I Wished on the Moon' allowed great freedom of movement to the front line of Goodman, Roy Eldridge and Ben Webster, and the result was vastly different from the background Goodman and the two Teagardens had provided for 'Riffin' the Scotch'. And in at least one of the four songs, 'I Wished on the Moon', there was that kind of melodic literacy and lyrical imagination that the singer's talent merited.

Now the formula for this session, being typical of all those that followed in the next three or four years, is worth examining in some detail. The first important point is that usually the songs were not those one would normally expect to find in the repertoire of the jazzman of the period, due, of course, to the insistence by the business interests involved that at least the titles should mean something to a public which had never heard of Billie Holiday or Teddy Wilson. So that songs like 'I Wished on the Moon' would have to be mugged up in the studio, there being no orchestration to hand upon which either the musicians or the singer cared to waste any breath.

In her autobiography, *Lady Sings the Blues*, Billie gives her own description of how these sessions were conducted. There are few more revealing passages in any book on jazz. The musicians arrived at the studio, sometimes not entirely sure who else was going to be there, but confident there would be no passengers. The selected song copy would be handed round, the chord sequence digested and the solos meted out. There was no music and very little plan. In other words, the recordings were quite plainly jazz performances which differed from the normal live session only in that they had to be restricted to three minutes playing time. In a most touching paragraph Billie bemoans the passing of the madcap days without seeming to realize why they were gone forever:

> On a recent date I tried to do it like the old days. I'd never seen the band or the arrangements, and I didn't know the songs they had picked for me, and they wanted me to do eight sides in three hours. We were doing all standards but nobody could read the stuff; the drummer did nothing but sit there grinning; the music had wrong chords; everybody was squawking. We pushed out about nine sides like they wanted. But not a damn one of them was any good.

The clue to the difference, not only between the early Billie sessions and the later albums, but between the entire jazz scene of, say, 1937 and 1957, is contained in that remarkable phrase of Billie's, 'the music had wrong chords'. In the sense in which Billie evidently meant it, there is literally no such thing as a wrong chord. I am not talking now of obvious solecisms like a major third in a minor triad, or the inclusion of the major seventh in a dominant seventh chord, but of altered chords, amended chords, substituted chords and the rest of the chromatic virtuosity which coloured the whole of jazz from the moment Parker and Gillespie forced themselves on to a world whose ear at first was too bigoted to listen.

The reason why the session Billie refers to was a failure had nothing to do with the ineptitude of the arrangers or indeed the grin of the drummer. It was linked to the fact that the kind of recordings for which Billie Holiday is now revered, required for their creation an implicit assumption on the part of the musicians taking part that no prearrangement was necessary because the harmonic conventions to which they were adhering were sufficiently limited to preclude any possibility of clash or confusion. The men who supported Billie in the early days were the most talented jazz musicians of their era. In such a situation, written arrangements would have been folly. The Swing Age was the last time in jazz history that the music was still free enough not to require the stratagems of prearrangement. Ten years later Sarah Vaughan could not do the same thing because by now the music had lost its innocence and demanded planning of the most detailed nature.

After the 'I Wished on the Moon' session, the recordings occurred regularly. A glance at the titles reveals that in theory both the singer and the instrumentalists should have been hamstrung by the mediocre quality of many of the songs. 'If You Were Mine' has a chord sequence well enough suited to the diatonic days of jazz, but the lyric is only passable. 'One, Two, Button Your Shoe' is a similar case, a reasonable harmonic structure but a lyric that is no more than an excuse for the counting-house gimmick. 'Me, Myself and I', 'If Dreams Come True', 'How Could You', were none of them bad tunes, but hardly the kind of material to inspire a great artist to great performances.

Sometimes her luck was better. 'These Foolish Things', 'Body and Soul', 'More Than You Know', 'You Go To My

Head' and 'Easy Living' represent the higher musical reaches of the Holiday discography. But when one listens to all these recordings indiscriminately, the skilful songs and the average jingles, the peculiar truth emerges that for some reason they were all more or less as good as each other, that apparently Billie Holiday was independent of the material she used. Songs came to her as competent minor products of the popular music machine of the day went through the treatment, and emerged as the touching expression of thoughts and emotions their composers had never dreamed of. 'Me Myself and I' sung by anyone else would be no more than the slightly cretinous but not objectionable expression of the infatuation of one person for another. The Billie Holiday recording is positively joyous. It abounds with the expression of a happy, helpless love, so that the triteness of the lyric disappears to be replaced by a wit of expression whose incongruity with the original tune is almost comical.

The process is even more impressive when it takes place in a worthier song. Billie Holiday's 'Summertime', recorded with an Artie Shaw struggling desperately and not quite successfully to be a big bad jazzman, possesses a quality of worldliness which no other recording of the song remotely approaches. The poesy of Ira Gershwin is transmuted into the realist expression of something more resilient. 'Your daddy's rich and your ma is good lookin' ', has a mature felicity about it that somehow enhances the phrase beyond all measure, reducing the conventional pseudo-operatic interpretation of the song to mere pap.

The same is true of 'Body and Soul' which, although it departs from the small jazz group formula of the other records, is identical in its vocal freedom. When Billie sings the words, she invests them with an intensity achieved by the childishly simple device of singing them as though she meant them. The fact that she chooses to sing the lesser-known alternate lyrics on the last middle eight, the lines that begin, 'What lies before me, a future that's stormy?' suggests that she must have given close thought to the meaning of the words before singing them.

The woman herself was inclined to be a little disingenuous about this autobiographical facet of her art. 'I've been told that nobody sings the word "hunger" like I do. Or the word "love". Maybe I remember what those words are all about.' What she means is that she knows very well that the overtones of a tragic personal life obtrude into every performance, but the curious thing is that these are not the only overtones. In some way suggestions of sweetness and light also become noticeable whenever she approaches a certain phrase or cadence.

There are two recordings from this period alive with optimism and bravery of spirit. Neither 'Without Your Love' nor 'Laughing At Life' sounds like the kind of song to defy the years. The lyrics in each case are competently constructed, and 'Without Your Love' has a few couplets easier to criticize than they are to compose. However, anyone who looked through the song copy would expect no more than a passable vocal performance. Billie Holiday invests it with an astonishing vitality that cannot be explained away by technical analysis. Her first chorus is comparatively subdued, and gives way to solos by Teddy Wilson and Buck Clayton. But when Billie returns for the last middle eight, the performance builds to an emotional climax in which the voice transforms the melody into an exultant cry. 'I'm like a plane without wings', sings Billie, and the written melody is almost abandoned. 'A violin with no strings', she continues, and the performance becomes a triumphal statement.

'Laughing At Life' is a valuable performance for rather different reasons. It demonstrates the nebulous process whereby an unplanned recording magically grows out of itself, so that in the end it does indeed have a form no less firm because apparently accidental. During the first vocal chorus Lester Young complements the vocal line with a certain phrase which later appears in the last chorus as a formal riff behind the voice. When it first appears, in Lester's first-chorus accompaniment to Billie, it appears to exist for a fleeting moment before subsiding. But the idea evidently stayed inside the head of Lester, because at the end he repeats the phrase after trimming it down. The other members of the band join in and the effect lifts the vocal up on its shoulders, so to speak. Had an orchestrator attempted something similar, the phrase would have lacked the light spontaneity of the version of 'Laughing With Life' we actually do possess. A successful jazz performance of this kind always lives on a knife-edge of failure until the very last cadence has been struck. The riff effect fitting so happily behind the vocal is one of those thousand-to-one shots which come off more than once with Billie Holiday because of the superlative quality of the men supporting her.

Some of these recordings from Billie's early days rank as the best jazz of their era. If the lay world, so readily fobbed off with imbecile corruptions of the term 'jam session', really wants to discover something true about jazz, it has only to give a few hours of its time to the Wilson–Holiday recording of 'I Must Have That Man', a side which contains the very quintessence of the jazz of the period. The sentiment of Dorothy Fields' lyric is ideally suited to the tender disillusion of Billie's delivery, so constrained as she opens the first chorus. The vocal is followed by solos from Benny Goodman, Lester Young and Buck Clayton, which brings us to the most remarkable fact of all about this remarkable recording. Billie completes the first chorus, then retires in favour of the soloists. Despite the greatness of the musicians involved, the listener finds himself awaiting the return of the voice, a return that on this recording never comes. It is one of the most impressive tributes to her ability that Billie Holiday was able to form a link in a chain comprised of the most gifted musicians of the period without ever allowing the tension of the performance to sag. The essence of this whole group of recordings is that the voice, besides being preoccupied with second-class light verse, is also elevated to the status of featured instrumentalist. As soon as Billie changed the formula, as in time she did, something of the integrated purity of performance was lost.

Why was the formula ever changed at all? Presumably because the professional status of the artist herself was changing. The 'Summertime' session was the first to appear under the name, 'Billie Holiday and Her Orchestra', a studio fiction no doubt, but still some slight indication of the rising tide of recognition. That was in the summer of 1936, and by the spring of the following year, another session under the same official heading is beginning to show signs of an evolution away from the small informal jam session of earlier days. On 'Where Is the Sun' and 'I Don't Know If I'm Coming or Going', the instrumentation is almost identical but the musicians are cast in a far more subservient role. There is little solo time for any of them, for the performance begins and ends with the vocal, now the chief attraction.

But the change was gradual and did not become the rule for some time yet. Indeed, the greatest triumphs of the informal sessions were still to come. January 25th, 1937, was a key date in jazz history because it was the first time that Billie Holiday and Lester Young recorded together. So monumental were the achievements of this partnership that we are now half-inclined to regard this whole pre-war era as one in which Billie and Lester were perpetually working together in the studios. In fact, it was not till Billie had been recording for three years that Lester made his appearance in her discography, by which time the formula for the unrehearsed method had already been evolved. Lester was not always available, possibly because of the touring commitments of the Basie band, but from now on, whenever it was possible, he appeared on every Wilson–Holiday recording date. It is worth remembering that recognition of Lester's talent was still rare in those days, another hint as to the instinctive musical acumen of a woman with no formal training or instrumental experience.

On the very first session they shared, the results were outstanding. Apart from 'I Must Have That Man', so typical of the best jazz of the day, there was 'He Ain't Got Rhythm', a little-known song of Irving Berlin's, on which Lester played one of the most cunningly wrought solos of his life. The lyric happened to possess just that degree of piquancy that Billie's voice could express so naturally. The time values she gives to the word 'equator' and her slightly unusual pronunciation of 'aviator' with which it rhymes, makes the whole phrase sound far wittier than it really is. Billie's insistence that her phrasing was strongly influenced by Lester's instrumental mannerisms is borne out by another track from the same session, 'This Year's Kisses', where Lester states the melody with that bland elegance reflected later when Billie starts to sing.

From then on, the Billie–Lester antiphonies flowed from the studios with astonishing consistency. 'I'll Never Be the Same' is one of the most skilful of all because it demonstrates a facet of the Holiday style that may have been born of either of two factors, or perhaps a combination of both. Instead of singing the written melody over the first two bars of the second half of the first chorus, Billie dispenses with the phrase, which is unexpectedly chromatic, employing instead a simple device of her own. The whole impact of the first phrase is changed. In the original the line 'I'll Never Be the Same' contains a furious activity, but Billie amends it to a single note repeated to accommodate the syllables of the phrase. It was a similar gambit to the one she used in 'I'll Get By', recorded earlier the same year, although the latter was so drastically amended that for a bar or two one is not quite sure she is not singing a different song from the one named on the label. Now this paraphrasing of the written melody in an instrumental manner was sometimes due to the limitations of her range. 'I'll Get By', for instance, has unusually generous intervals spanning its opening few bars, and it is very possible that Billie Holiday, always very much a middle-of-the-register singer, felt more comfortable compressing the range of the song rather than impose upon herself the slightest element of the wrong kind of strain, or have the musicians fishing around for appropriate keys. On the other hand, I believe that the kind of paraphrase to be found in 'I'll Never Be the Same', which typifies all her work, has artistic rather than technical origins. Billie Holiday was removing the odium of a slightly precocious phrase, replacing it with one that is alive with all the candour and apparent simplicity of much of the best jazz.

There is one recording from this period where the considerations of range really did cause her some hard thinking, so that on 'I Cried For You', encompassing a jump of a major ninth in its first three bars, the group plays jazz first. Johnny Hodges gives a masterly statement of the theme which departs from the written line without ever ceasing to pay it deference, before Teddy Wilson plays an impeccable four-bar modulation taking the key down a minor third for the convenience of the singer. Somebody like Sarah Vaughan would never have to resort to such tactics, which is why she is able to sing a tune like 'Poor Butterfly', again with a demanding range, without resorting to the anti-climactic device of dropping down an octave to avoid a crisis of pitch. But what handicap is a restricted range when the act of compression can achieve such felicities as the remoulding of the first phrase of 'I'll Never Be the Same' or the complete recasting of the melodic line of 'I'll Get By'?

Much later in her career, when the ravages of a desperately unhappy life were beginning to tell, her range shrank much more seriously, so that in singing old stand-bys like 'Body and Soul' and 'These Foolish Things', she dropped her key by a tone or sometimes more. But by then her voice had changed so profoundly in character that she was a different kind of artist altogether. The great virtue of the recordings from the first period was their heart-lifting optimism, a certain buoyancy of spirit which made the listener feel an affinity for a disembodied sound whose owner he might never have heard of before. I am convinced that for much of the time Billie was not consciously aware of what she was doing while she was doing it. To her, singing was not so much the exercise of an artistic function as the natural means of expression towards the world. This relationship involving the mechanics of making music is common enough among the best instrumentalists, but certainly no singer since Bessie Smith could be said to need to sing as desperately as Billie Holiday. The casual effects she threw off would be psychological masterstrokes had they been thought out and planned ahead. As it was, they remained emphatic triumphs of intuition.

One of the most affecting examples occurs in the Holiday recording of 'What Shall I Say?', a deceptively simple-sounding little melody with one of those invisible dynamos built into it so that one has only to play it as written with a modicum of rhythmic understanding to produce a reasonable jazz performance. In the lyric the following lines occur:

> *What shall I say when the phone rings*
> *and somebody asks for you?*
> *They don't know I ask for you too.*
> *What shall I say?*

The vowel sounds at the end of the second and third lines could be awkward to sing. The word 'you' is included twice, but with obviously different stresses, and at very different points in the line. Moreover, the second 'you' occurs immediately before the word rhyming with the first 'you'. It is not a clumsily written lyric, but it might have been constructed with rather more consideration for the singer than the writer has shown. There are a dozen ways round the problem. Billie Holiday's is the best, as well as the simplest of all. She pronounces the first 'you' in the normal way, doing the same with the word 'too' which rhymes with it. The second 'you' she simply changes to 'ya', thus eliminating any danger of idiotically echoing vowel sounds.

But the mere technical process is not what is important. Probably Billie never even considered it. She must have come to the amendment of the second 'you' by an entirely different path, and when we listen to the recording it is very obvious where that path lay. When that second 'you' occurs, changed to a 'ya', the whole performance suddenly stops being a formal musical exercise and instead confronts the listener with a human statement, directed specifically at whoever happens to be present. There is an amazing colloquial candour about that second 'you', born of the ability of the woman singing it to make the tritest lyric a valid statement of emotional experience. When 'ya' appears, one suddenly realizes with a disturbed shock of surprise, that Billie is experiencing the lyric dramatically as well as musically, so that the finished product has a depth of sensitivity unknown to other women singers since Bessie Smith.

Sometimes the ability to make a certain phrase, or word, or perhaps just a syllable, shine with a fresh lustre, seems to be a lucky shot in the dark, but it is really part of a system no less comprehensive because it happens to be subconscious. Billie Holiday, who never suggested she might know of factors in a poetic performance like mantic overtones, had an infallible instinct for evoking these overtones every time she stepped up to a microphone. In 'Blame it on the Weather', an obscure pop song recorded in January 1939, with Wilson, Benny Carter and Roy Eldridge, she sings the phrase, 'they'll see through me like glass', delivering the last word in such a way as to rehabilitate it, investing it with all its translucent qualities. The word flashes and shimmers with a crystalline brilliance, transmuting a commonplace simile into a shaft of genuine poetry. This ability to restore to tired words the vitality they once had, abounds throughout her work and is the key to several truths about her style, especially its inimicability.

There are surprisingly few instances where she actually creates a specific melodic phrase of the kind one used to find in the quaint old series, 'Fifty Hot Licks'. Her improvisations can hardly ever be torn out of context because they are rather affairs of stresses of syllables, subtleties of phrasing, regrouping of notes. None of her inventions are as elaborate or as ambitious as, say, Sarah Vaughan's celebrated version of 'Body and Soul', which is better compared with instrumental versions like those of Hawkins and Red Allen than it is with Billie Holiday's. The Sarah Vaughan 'Body and Soul' is highly ingenious rather than inspired. It accepts the challenge of modern harmony with brilliant resource, but it reeks of the midnight oil in a way that none of Billie Holiday's performances ever did. The difference between them is the difference between a perfect abstraction and a slice of humanism.

Now and then a whole phrase does leap out of its context into the memory purely as a fragment of musical invention, like the rephrasing of the notes of 'a telephone that rings' in the 1952 version of 'These Foolish Things', recorded with one of the JATP concert parties. More typical is the way she remoulds an entire song, flattening a phrase here, stretching a

time value there, reducing the arpeggio phrases to the very
bone, slipping in a grace note which just so happens to be one
of the most important harmonies of the chord.

In 'One Two, Button Your Shoe', made in the vintage
days with Bunny Berigan and Irving Fazola, she virtually
abandons the written line completely, using the harmonies
whose names she did not know, to build a new, sleeker
melodic line which reduced the number of pitches by more
than half, until a phrase like 'tell me you get a thrill', originally linked syllable by syllable to the arpeggio of the major
seventh with the major sixth thrown in to make up the
number, emerges through the voice simply as the actual note
of the major seventh and not its arpeggio, repeated four
times, exactly as Lester Young might have played it, or any
competent jazzman of experience. The next phrase is identical except that the major seventh chord now becomes the
dominant seventh, whereupon Billie promptly performs the
same trick a semitone lower, giving form to her variations
just as though she had swotted up the harmonies from the
textbooks the night before, when really she is trusting to her
ear and her taste.

No jazz musician, whether he uses his vocal chords or an
instrumental keyboard, can be taught this kind of invention.
It is the fruit of instinct wedded to experience, and therefore
remains exclusively the possession of the man who spends
most of his life weaving instrumental patterns round chord
sequences. From people with no instrumental training it is
unfair even to expect it, which is why Billie Holiday is
unique in all the annals of jazz.

Because of the apparently nebulous nature of this art of
making jazz, a process impossible to convey by teaching or by
writing down in congruous terms, or even recognizable without a certain sympathy in the mind and heart of the observer,
there are very few technicalities by which the theorists can

blind us with their science when discussing Billie Holiday's singing. M. Hodeir may potter about indefinitely preaching to the converted and terrifying everybody else by the diabolonian cunning with which he computes the mathematical processes which go into the making of a jazz record, but his method founders in the face of a performance by Billie Holiday. There is nothing to compute, no inversions to detect, no daring passing chords to recognize by name, none of the contents of the usual box of vocal tricks which may easily be defined according to the rules of discord and resolution. There are a few Holiday mannerisms reducible to academic terms, but far less than in the case of the two contemporaries whom most people mistakenly regard as her closest rivals, Ella Fitzgerald and Sarah Vaughan.

One habit in particular of Billie's has a wry relevance to her art because many people who know of it misconstrue it as a serious deficiency and even a source of embarrassment. On recordings spanning her entire career, Billie has a habit of falling away from the pitch of a note soon after she arrives at it. I have heard this device cited as proof of her inability to hold a note long enough to establish its pitch. But the musician who listens carefully to these falls soon notices that far from being technical solecisms, they are musically correct effects enhancing the dramatic impact of the lyric. It is not by accident that every time Billie falls away from these notes, she allows the fall to continue just so far and then arrests it—at the next note down in the arpeggio of the relevant chord. She was especially partial to this effect when the chord in question was a diminished seventh, probably because her instinct told her that the intervals between the notes of that chord, all minor thirds, were not so broad that they might sound too protracted. This fall is one of her devices in the transmutation of 'I'll Never Be the Same', on the phrase, 'a lot that a smile may hide'.

However, this description of what is after all an elementary trick of improvisation does not do justice to the artist, because once again the device was a means to an end, the end being the expression of a kind of fatality in the world she sang about. The fall would express a wry sense of philosophic despair, as though even the happy songs were wise in the knowledge of sadder lyrics and sadder lives. There is a profound difference between this kind of stylistic sophistication and the harmonic dexterity of Ella Fitzgerald which, being an end in itself, finally reduces the art of singing to the decadence of gibberish. Instead of aspiring to establish the voice as a second-class instrumental keyboard, the singer should attempt to raise it to the highest jazz level because of its potential value in expressing specific ideas and emotions rather than the impressionistic gestures of most instrumental jazz. The gibberish vocal makes a mockery of communication instead of exalting it. The thought of Billie Holiday indulging in such antics is too far from reality to be considered for more than a moment. It is useless your analysts telling you that Ella Fitzgerald or Sarah Vaughan can follow the most intricate chord sequence through to the ultimate flattened fifth in the final tonic chord, hitting resolution after resolution with the same correctitude as any suburban music teacher. When the emotional content is nil, all the correctitude in the world will not save the performance from artistic damnation, an observation that applies more than ever in the world of modern jazz, with its daunting harmonic complexities and its pathetic pursuit of legitimate acceptance.

In the early 1940s Billie Holiday's career entered on the second of its three phases. Gradually the small-group formula was cast aside, being replaced by an accompanying orchestra playing decorous arrangements, neatly rehearsed and carefully tailored to meet the demands of the singer. The implication was quite clear. Billie Holiday was now the star.

No longer was she one of a group of jazzmen creating variations on written themes. The voice was now the focal point, apart from a few fragments thrown the way of the soloist, like Roy Eldridge's masterly eight bars in 'Body and Soul', used as a buffer between the end of the first chorus and the introduction into the performance of the alternate lyrics to the middle eight. From the purist point of view these recordings have nothing like the value of the earlier masterpieces, which had Billie to offer and half a dozen others besides. But judged strictly as vocal performances they show no noticeable decline from the sessions of the middle 1930s.

I mention 'Mandy is Two' because it bears such forcible testimony to Billie's talent for endowing any old jingle with the grace of art. The lyric is a piece of sentimentality of the worst kind, difficult to endure without resort to rabelaisian noises. Its conquest by Billie Holiday is symbolic of her whole career. By showing she could make such songs valid in the jazz context, she was demonstrating in the most dramatic way that there is no material that cannot be used as jazz material if the artist involved is gifted enough, and that triteness itself, pitifully inferior to the realist beauty of the words Bessie Smith sang, may be invested with an emotional depth to move the most hardened of cynics.

Billie, was, in fact, annexing a huge area of musical experience on behalf of jazz. She was reclaiming all the land of the popular song. Of course she was not the first to attempt this. Musicians had been borrowing silly jingles and making great jazz out of them for two generations. She was not even the first singer to do this. Louis Armstrong had actually made 'Song of the Islands' sound something like the real thing. But Billie was the first figure in jazz whose entire career was concerned with this type of performance of this type of material. She was dealing in the medium of words all the time, so that no matter how prejudiced you might be towards jazz, no matter how indifferent you were to the pathos of its cadences, you could at least understand what it was this woman was singing about.

Usually she was singing about love, one of the two subjects in the world about which everybody in the world professes to be an expert. (The other is music.) She took these songs far more seriously than anyone else dreamed of doing. To other singers they were the excuse for standing up and simulating a few emotional platitudes. To audiences they bore no relationship to reality at all, being the incidental music of a dream world where unrequited love wept crocodile tears, all expressed in mediocre verse. To the men who wrote the songs, they were factory products, designed to live for a few moments and then be cast aside, so that their component parts might be broken down and redesigned in fresh permutations. When Billie Holiday hit upon songs like 'I've Got A Date With a Dream' or 'Please Keep Me in Your Dreams' the tunesmiths of Tin Pan Alley got more than they had ever bargained for and certainly more than they deserved.

The use of more formal musical settings for her recordings raises a point about Billie Holiday which may never effectively be answered. In 1941 Lester Young made his last recordings with her. Many factors must have contributed towards this split. It was the period when Lester was severing his connections with the Basie band. It was also the time when Billie was sufficiently established, at least with a small coterie audience, to record under her own name. And possibly more important than either of these factors, the Swing Age was slowly grinding to a halt. In retrospect we can see quite clearly that during the early 1940s the Wilson–Young–Eldridge axis was gradually being replaced as the advance guard of jazz. The arrivistes Parker and Gillespie were soon to make the work of the Wilson generation so quaint in its comparative innocence that its eventual appeal was destined to be the elusive charm of a period piece. The era of the small jazz group busking away in the recording studio without much of a plan to guide the musicians, was slowly becoming no more than a glorious chapter of the past.

However, the assessment of these factors soon becomes impossible, because the most dominant fact of all is one which by its very nature cannot be measured with any accuracy. The romance between Billie and Lester is one of those rare exquisite moments when melodrama and prosaic reality reach out and touch for a while. It is a truism of jazz history that the partnership with Lester Young, personal as well as professional, was the most vital association of Billie Holiday's career. It proved to be a working romance which was unusually fruitful, as connoisseurs well know. Were its two central figures artists of the same magnitude in any other sphere, then the task of the biographer would be eased considerably. But the mature approach to this kind of situation is consistently lacking in the jazz world, almost as though in the final reckoning the musicians were too self-conscious about the artistic possibilities of what they were doing to accept their own place with complete *savoir-faire*. It is understandable enough that nobody will ever read *The Collected Letters of Billie Holiday* or *The Private Correspondence of Lester Young*, so it is left for the curious to wonder about the possible clues to the nature of the close friendship of the period's most remarkable singer and instrumentalist.

It is too tempting to draw the obvious conclusions, to say that the two careers became one and were therefore never the same after the parting. Or that Lester's uncanny knack of complementing Billie's vocal phrases with his own aphorisms was the result not just of musical instinct, but of musical instinct enhanced by the passion of a love affair. There is a remarkable parallelism in both the rate and nature of their artistic declines that might be more than coincidence. But, then, Lester's oblique instrumental comments on a vocal performance may just as easily be found behind Jimmie Rushing as Billie Holiday, and nobody has suggested that Lester ever felt unduly romantic about Jimmie Rushing. What failure there was in the careers of each of them seems to have been a failure of temperament, not the failure to meet a romantic crisis.

Neither Lester nor Billie said anything very substantial about the effect of their relationship on their work together. Each one bore for the rest of his professional career the nickname the other concocted, and Billie did say, several times, that she always felt happier about a session when she knew Lester would be present. In her own words:

> For my money Lester was the world's greatest. I loved his music, and some of my favourite recordings are the ones with Lester's pretty solos. . . . Lester sings with his horn; you listen to him and can almost hear the words. People think he's so cocky and secure, but you can hurt his feelings in two seconds. I know, because I found out once that I had. We've been hungry together, and I'll always love him and his horn.

Her reference to the vocal overtones of Lester's style establishes beyond reasonable doubt that there was some artistic as well as emotional interdependence. Lester's whimsy about always thinking of the lyrics to a song when you were improvising on it, is worth considering also. It is fair to assume that on recordings like 'Laughing At Life', 'Without Your Love', 'Me, Myself and I', 'Mean To Me' and 'Time On My Hands', on all of which Lester displays an instinct for what Billie is going to sing that is almost psychic, there were moments where the warmth of a private liaison spilled over on to the grooves of the record. Whatever anyone cares to imagine, the antiphony they created remains un-matched in all jazz, ranking among the rarest delights the music has to offer.

The tragic decline of Billie Holiday's fortunes in the last years of her life is another of those commonplaces of jazz criticism about which nothing new of any relevance to the music can be said. The same element of self-destruction that shadowed the life of Charlie Parker is evident in Billie's career. Nobody has any illusions about the terrifying inroads on her talent made by the way she chose to live.

Because her recognition, like Lester's, was a belated one, there is a tendency to revere anything she did in the last years of her life, to ignore conveniently the fact that by the middle 1950s she had hardly any voice left at all. This decay may be charted in every detail throughout the recordings she has left us, but before it began to be serious, and after the break with Lester, she cut several more outstanding tracks, in some of which can be noted a brave attempt to behave as though time were not racing ahead at all. The sessions with Eddie Hey-wood are a case in point. 'How Am I To Know' shows her amending arpeggio phrases once again into a flatter line while still suggesting the framework of the original tune by stressing the more prominent of the harmonies. 'I'll Be See-ing You' shows how she could take a popular ballad, ad-mittedly of a superior kind, and transform it into something so touching that nobody who knows the recording can take anyone else's version very seriously.

'On the Sunny Side of the Street', recorded with a rhythm section led by Heywood in April 1944, demonstrates the instrumental nature of her thought. The opening phrases of the first theme, containing the words, 'Take your coat and take your hat', and 'Can't you hear that pitter pat?', make use of only three notes in the diatonic scale, and are reminiscent of the remarkable phrase Lester played in his Aladdin recording of the same song a little later, when he makes a fall of an octave in the most unexpected place.

Throughout the 1940s Billie continued to make records which although they were distinct in character from the pre-war hit-or-miss classics, were unmatched in their field, then and now. The more commercial nature of the orchestral backing may have won them a slightly wider fringe audience that she usually commanded, but the songs themselves compromise not a single crotchet in their suitability to her style. 'Good Morning, Heartache', with its rise from minor to major in its first eight bars, is typical Holiday material. But the side I usually associate with this period and this type of recording is 'Crazy He Calls Me', which, besides having an amusing lyric and an unusual melodic line, happens to possess a certain relevance to Billie's attitude towards her lovers in private life. In 'Lady Sings the Blues', there is more than one echo of the futile devotion of this song.

The divine spark died very hard. Almost to the end she was capable of producing the kind of vocal vitality that can carry an entire accompanying group, as she did in a heroic version of 'All Of Me', recorded with one of the earliest JATP groups. As late as 1955 in 'Please Don't Talk About Me When I'm Gone', she eclipses Benny Carter, Harry Edison and Barney Kessell in the buoyancy of her delivery, producing another colloquial effect that lends an unexpected edge to the words. At the opening of the second eight she sings 'listen', dropping the second syllable an octave in a manner so casual that for a moment the performance ceases to be vocal and becomes speech instead. Both these tracks revive to some extent the glories of earlier times, with their rough insistence that jazz is a down-to-earth affair, making a strange contrast with the tonal felicities of Sarah Vaughan's commercial output and Ella Fitzgerald's faithful deadpan transcriptions of the Songbooks.

147

In the last two or three years of her life the songs she chose
to record were usually sad ballads whose lyrics time and
again forced even the most objective of listeners to see the
parallels with her private life, for by now her technique was
so ravaged by physical decline that she was by all the normal
rules, no longer qualified to sing any song demanding sus-
tained notes and skilled control. But the normal rules applied
to her no more at the end of her life than they had in the
beginning. Whatever shortcomings there might now be in her
breathing, her range and her pronunciation, she had retained,
because it was a very real part of her personality, this unfailing ability to wrest out of every lyric the last drop of significance, and even to insert her own where the lyricist had
failed to include it. As this was the very core of her art, the
last recordings overcame their own technical limitations in a
miraculous way.

The British edition of 'The Billie Holiday Memorial'
issued by Fontana, inadvertently demonstrates this. The
album is made up of recordings from the pre-war period,
except for the last track of all, made within a year of her death
'For All We Know' is yet another song whose lyrics might be
a personal statement as well as a vocal recitation. At first the
contrast between this croaking, middle-aged voice and the
purity of the young hopeful girl of 'On the Sentimental Side'
is truly frightening. It all sounds like a clinical demonstration
of the suffering and unhappiness of a woman whose life
ended in circumstances as wretched as any person's could.
There seems to be nothing left of a wonderful talent. But
more detailed listening suggests that in its way, 'For All We
Know' is the most moving statement on the whole album,
not simply the grisly evidence of the decline and fall of a
once-great artist.

All the ballad performances of these last years must be
approached in the same way. They must not be evaluated

according to the normal rules of the vocal game, because to Billie Holiday it never was a game. Whether or not she was able to curb her mannerisms of style, now becoming parodies of themselves, whether or not she was aware she might be making a public confessional of her own decay, whether or not her breath was too short and the bar-lengths too long, or the control of her now drunken vibrato painfully ineffectual, she knew she was echoing the same lyrical sentiments she had expressed twenty-five years before. The raw material of the words had maintained their constancy, while the most vital facet of her art, the ability to make those lyrics sound profound, had not deserted her.

Performances like 'For All We Know' must therefore be accepted as recitative with musical accompaniment rather than as ordinary singing. This is admittedly special pleading but it is entered on behalf of a very special jazz musician, and is in fact perfectly justified. It is always disastrous to present a record like 'For All We Know' to somebody who, being unaware of the details of the life and career of the singer, merely accepts it as another song by another crooner and finds, quite naturally, that the performance is excruciatingly bad, just as a prospective furniture buyer seeking polished walnut would recoil in horror from the trunk of an oak tree. By the criteria of that person, Billie's voice would impress only by its complete inadequacy to cope with technical problems that half the technicoloured sopranos of Hollywood could master without a thought, and usually do.

But Billie's technical decline did not matter. In a way it actually made her one supreme virtue more evident than ever. At the very end she was barely capable of singing at all in the conventional sense. Her range had shrunk to unmanageable proportions. Her diction unconsciously parodied the girlish delights of the 1930s. Her breathing was laboured. Of actual tunefulness, melodiousness, or whatever we care to call the beguiling rise and fall of the line of a melody, there was almost none.

The trappings were stripped away, but where the process would normally leave only the husk of a fine reputation, it only exposed to view, once and for all, the true core of her art, her handling of a lyric. If the last recordings are approached with this fact in mind, they are seen to be, not the insufferable croakings of a woman already half-dead, but recitatives whose dramatic intensity becomes unbearable, statements as frank and tragic as anything throughout the whole range of popular art.

In view of this, it is understandable that the more ambitious the lyric, the more effective its delivery by Billie Holiday was likely to be, and that any song involving the pathos of pastness, the relentless advance of time and nostalgic understanding of the transient nature of experience, would sorely tempt us to equate it with the facts of Billie's life. Thus, 'Speak Low', a song of rare sensitivity in its approach to the subject of the transience of love, takes on a further dimension when Billie sings it, becoming an authentic statement by the middle-aged on the brevity of youth. Each of the phrases, 'Everything ends, the curtain descends', 'love is pure gold and time a thief', 'our summer day withers away', 'our moment is swift', and above all the reiteration of the phrase 'too soon' spring to life as they do under the touch of no other singer. So does one come across Don Pedro's words, 'Speak low if you speak love' from *Much Ado About Nothing*, through the medium of jazz music and a dying woman. The depth of the performance is here indisputable, as we forget for a moment about singing in its conventional technical sense and hear instead someone using the jazz idiom to convey, subconsciously or otherwise the story of a life which, for all its towering artistic achievements, was ravaged by self-indulgence and finally destroyed by drug addiction.

Billie Holiday's gift of treating a lyric leads us finally to the most daunting speculation of all. If her touch was infallible, as it certainly seems to have been, what might have happened had the songs of her life been cast more artistically, or written with a finer sensitivity, or dealt with a range of subjects a little broader than the encroaching horizons of unrequited love? Naturally there must have been a limit to the range and depth of her expression, which was no doubt suitably employed when singing of the love of a woman for a man. Such themes were the very quiddity of her personality. But there is one incident in her career that gives us a strong hint of what might have been, where the lyric moves away for a moment from the boudoir and the 'two-by-four' she sings of in 'He's Funny That Way', and concerns itself with one of the crucial themes of the twentieth century.

Most of Billie's best-known songs concern the inhumanity of men towards women. 'Strange Fruit' deals with the inhumanity of man towards man. It is a bitter and ironic comment on a race murder, worlds removed from the asinine demi-monde of gay amours and faithless lovers to which most popular singers are committed. Much is written about jazz as the music of social protest, but it is sometimes difficult today to see how it is protesting, or what it is protesting about, and to whom, especially now that it has purchased, at the price of its own blood, an evening dress suit, swopping its candour for respectability. In 'Strange Fruit' the mask is off and for a few minutes jazz is being specific.

I do not know whether, according to the peculiar lights of the purists, 'Strange Fruit' by Billie Holiday is a jazz record. I do not know, or care, whether there are those who will shuffle uncomfortably and point out that 'Strange Fruit' is politically 'committed', and therefore no work of art at all. What I do know is that it would have been lamentable had a woman of her talent not grappled at least once in her life

151

with so universal a theme. In so doing, she proved yet again that jazz music can extend its boundaries far wider than many of its patrons realize, and that there is literally no subject not fair game for the jazz singer provided she happens to be a Bessie Smith or a Billie Holiday.

For the whole point about Billie's 'Strange Fruit' is that the effectiveness of the performance lies not in the lyric but in its expression by a jazz singer. The effect could only have been gained by an artist steeped in the very quintessence of the jazz art all her life. The rise and fall of the phrases, the shaping of the words, the feeling for a dying cadence and the occasional slight amendment or variation of the melody, these are the exclusive weapons of the jazz artist. No other musician can possibly have access to them. They are, indeed, all that the jazz musician has to offer the world of music at large, and they cannot be acquired to quite the same degree in any other kind of musical environment. Certainly they cannot be reduced to a formula and sold at a guinea an hour, as some musicians attempt to do. If the jazz musician, in his preoccupation with the conquest of harmony, forfeits these weapons, then he is behaving like the ship's captain who tore up the keel to make fuel for the engines.

I believe that when Billie Holiday sings the phrase 'pastoral scene of the gallant South', civilization has said its last word about the *realpolitik* of racial discrimination in all its forms and degrees. The resigned bitterness and contempt with which Billie throws out the phrase, leaves nothing else to be said. And the bitterness and contempt are rendered by someone who knew the hard truth of discrimination, even in its less deadly forms.

There was once a film produced in Hollywood called 'New Orleans'. It was no better and no worse than all the other films from Hollywood involving jazz music in one way or another. In other words it was an insult to reasonable intelligence, a slur upon the artistry of every jazz musician who ever strode from the dominant to the tonic without falling flat on his face, a lie sold to gullible audiences at two and threepence a throw. The plot has passed into merciful oblivion, where it came from in the first place, but one well-remembered detail is that the heroine was a great singer who had a ladies' maid. The great singer had a voice like an understudy at a suburban operatic society. The ladies' maid was played by Billie Holiday. The incident is humorously recounted in 'Lady Sings the Blues', and ends with the comment, 'I never made another movie. And I'm in no hurry'.

Her death occurred within a few months of the death of Lester Young, and since then the best work of both of them has been made available in Memorial albums. Valuable as these collections undoubtedly are, there is only one way to appraise Billie's career with any justice, the same way as one appraises Lester Young's, in strict chronological order. And at each stage of the journey, the listener should administer upon himself the corrective of the corresponding work of contemporaries like Goodman, Ellington, Hawkins and Basic.

This kind of diligence reveals the fairly natural division of the Holiday career into three parts; the first, covering roughly the pre-war period, produced infinitely the best jazz, largely because the conventions of the day were in perfect harmony with the talents of the musicians expressing them; the second saw Billie emerging as the leading attraction of each performance, eliminating a great deal of the instrumental virtuosity going on in the background; the third traced her melodramatic fall into a premature grave during a time when she recorded a series of vocal performances, hardly vocal performances at all, which, despite their academic crudities, stand as heart-searing evocations of the jazz spirit.

Throughout this career the material is drawn almost

exclusively from outside the jazz world, which is essentially an instrumental world and cannot by its very nature produce good vocal material, any more than a Beethoven can induce a trombone to deliver verbal addresses. For the strange truth is that theoretically there is no such thing as a jazz singer. The very phrase is a contradiction in terms. The reason is the same one as the reason why there is no such thing as a two-hundred-year-old man. It takes too long. Life is too short for the production of either phenomenon. The jazz singer, were she to exist, would have to have all the intimacy with the abstract world of harmonic patterns which only a practising instrumentalist can ever acquire. She must be able, not only to sense the dramatic beauty of the resolution of the dominant seventh chord built on the mediant of the scale, as Billie does when she reaches the second bar of 'On the Sunny Side of the Street', but to understand how such an an effect is achieved, when it is grammatically permissible to achieve it, and how best to adjust the time-values of the syllables of the lyric, if and when she meets the other requirements. For it is the grossest fallacy to regard a girl who sings merely as an instrumentalist who happens to be using her vocal chords instead of a keyboard. Singing of that kind, which Duke Ellington used to set up for Kay Davis, belongs in an entirely different category, one of relatively minor importance, by the very nature of the fact that the Kay Davis effect possesses neither the resonance of an instrument nor the ability to convey specific ideas through the medium of language.

In a way the singer has a far harder task than any instrumentalist. The player who would improvise is limited only by the movement of harmony from bar to bar. He can use as many or as few notes as he pleases, so long as he lives by the inexorable rules of resolution governing whichever convention of jazz he happens to have been raised on. Not so the singer who, in addition to her subservience to the harmonies, has also to pay tribute to the number of syllables in each bar. If she decides to defy the syllabic content, she finds herself faced with one of three dilemmas, each more terrifying than the other.

She may find herself obliged to stretch out a vowel sound like a piece of elastic, repeating it at several pitches until the time duration for that vowel sound is fulfilled. Ella Fitzgerald often does this, and although she does it with technical expertise, the point of the matter has not the remotest connection with technical expertise. If a singer indulges in the Elastic approach, she may, when singing 'All the Things You Are', find herself confronted with the awkward fact that the first word of the lyric, 'You', occupies the first four beats of the song, the whole first bar, so that if she is to attempt the same skill as the musician does, at shaping phrases based on a harmonic underpinning, she is going to have to keep saying the word 'you' until the first bar is over. If, as is likely, she discovers that the chord which gives light and shade to that word is the relative minor common chord of the key, she will very likely sing the three notes of that triad, top them off with the root an octave lower, allow one crotchet to each note, thus filling in the correct time value of her first bar, and intone the sound 'Yoo-Hoo-Hoo-Hoo'. As instrumental jazz the effect is poor. As vocal jazz it is even worse, because it is placing an inoffensive little vowel sound on the rack of protraction and keeping it there until the metronome sounds the moment of release.

Very often the singer, who works her way into this beguiling but deadly trap, makes a desperate attempt to work her way out of it again by finally refusing to acknowledge the sovereignty of words at all. Now she is free. Now she can create patterns in no way inferior to the creations of musicians, except that, lacking the experience and craftsmanship which comes with the struggle for mastery over a tangible keyboard, she will lack also the good taste that usually comes with this ability. But at least she is now free. At what cost? A hair-raising one, reduction of the English language to absurdity, all on the pretext of making the human voice sound like an instrument. Singers who really desire the status of an instrument should stop making life difficult for themselves and everyone else within earshot, and learn to play one, just as the reactionaries who insist that every instrumentalist ought to simulate the sound of the human voice should have their vocal chords removed and a trombone rammed down their gullets instead.

Gibberish vocals are the price the singer has to pay for this freedom to move about the realms of discord and resolution without the attendant drudgery of keyboard practice. No matter whether the gibberish is grammatically correct as with Ella Fitzgerald, or positively ingenious, as with Sarah Vaughan, it will still be gibberish whose emotive content is roughly nil, because it is hampered by all the drawbacks of the voice in jazz while abandoning its one great advantage, the achievement of catharsis through the use of familiar words and familiar combinations of words.

There is a third way by which the singer might grant herself this limitless freedom without resorting to gibberish, and that is to sing original lyrics to her own improvisations, always keeping in mind the distinction between the authentic jazz vocal and all other variations, from the recitation of jazz-with-poetry to nonsensical shooby-dooby tongue-wagging. The distinction to this. The jazz vocal, if it is not to deliquesce into a gooey pool at the singer's feet, must for most of the time have one verbal sound for each note. The first bar of 'All the Things You Are', which has one note, has only one syllable, while the first bar of 'Carolina in the Morning', whose number of beats is the same, comprises, not one semibreve but eight quavers, and has therefore been provided, most thoughtfully, by Gus Kahn with the eight vowel sounds, 'Nothing could be fi-ner than to'.

It is now that the enormity of what Billie Holiday was attempting begins to become apparent. For the last of the three alternatives, the composition of the singer's own words to match the movements of her own improvisations, has two painful riders. First, she must take care never to be manoeuvred into an impromptu performance, because she must always be limited to the number of verbal compositions she has managed to complete. Second, she had better have the skill of the lyricists whose words she is superseding, if she is not to be jeered out of court for vandalism. Annie Ross half-managed to do this, but her best recordings were not wholly self-supporting because the starting-point was always somebody else's solo, in its way more disastrous than trying to improve on Ira Gershwin and Lorenz Hart. There can have been few more telling exhibitions of inadvertent musical folly than Jon Hendrick's diseased-hip lyrics to Charlie Parker's solo on 'Now's the Time'. Anita O'Day will be remembered as the brave spirit who attempted a jazzbo-doggerel edition of Cole Porter's lyrics to 'You're the Top'. The double-talk marathons of Ella Fitzgerald and Sarah Vaughan, amusing and skilful though they may be, have nothing to do with the art of remoulding a melody without at the same time strangling its lyric.

What has all this to do with Billie Holiday? Everything, because she happens to have been the only woman singer of the past thirty years who achieved the impossible. Unless we understand what she was attempting, we cannot attempt to decide whether she succeeded and whether it was worth succeeding at. By a fortuitous combination of natural endowment and accidental circumstance, of environment and heredity, she actually did possess this rarest of all jazz instincts, the sense of form. She may have acquired it through early indoctrination with the work of Louis Armstrong and Bessie Smith. She may have inherited it from her father, Clarence Holiday, who once worked in the Fletcher Henderson Orchestra. Probably she was born with it. She was that freak thing, the born or natural musician. Had she been a man, she would surely have taken to instrumental improvisation as naturally as Teddy Wilson did, or Lester Young or any of the rest of her early collaborators. It is impossible to teach a girl what Billie could do, and even if it were it would take a lifetime to teach it. She just happened to have the natural musician's ear for harmonic movement combined with the actor's aptitude for word combinations. Plunged as she was, virtually from birth, into a jazz environment, her singing possessed an extraordinary validity intensified by the fact that throughout a tempestuous life she experienced on a personal level all the situations used as themes in the lyrics of the songs she sang.

That is why it is artistic suicide for any other singer to attempt a facsimile, even were she to possess the same musical instinct. Billie Holiday's great performances are the fruit of her experience of her own life. The performances of her imitators are the fruit of their experience of Billie Holiday.

6

‹›››‹‹‹›

CHARLIE PARKER

'. . . the technical history of modern harmony is a history of growth of toleration by the human ear of chords that at first sounded discordant and senseless to the main body of contemporary professional musicians.'

BERNARD SHAW

THE advent of Charlie Parker caused more violent irruptions, more bitterness, more sheer apoplectic rage than that of any jazz musician before him. Before he happened, there was no serious split down the middle of the jazz ranks. After he arrived, it was no longer sufficient to claim you were a jazz fan. The term no longer had a precise or narrow meaning. It was now necessary to qualify the claim, to explain what kind of jazz fan you were, to commit yourself either to the music that was pre-Charlie Parker or the music he was playing. From now on there were to be two quite distinct jazz worlds, the ancient and the modern, and in the cut-and-thrust of the war which followed it escaped the notice of most people, musicians included, that it was by no means obligatory to choose one side or the other. Even in later years, when Parker's neologisms became standard jazz practice, the jazz-lover of catholicity who made no secret of his admiration both of Armstrong and Parker was aware he was admiring two very different kinds of music.

The difficulty now confronts the commentator of Charlie Parker's career that it is literally impossible to say anything about its revolutionary nature without restoring to technical terms, a fact which in itself ought to give a broad hint as to what the fuss was all about. The phrase 'technical terms' only sounds forbidding, of course, to those who possess no musical faculty apart from the instincts of their ears, sometimes prodigious. But to ask anybody to write about the nebulous processes of musical improvisation without at times resorting to technicalities is to ask him to make bricks without straw. After all, the technicalities themselves are no more advanced academically than, say, third year French grammar. It is only because so many people lacked the energy to acquaint themselves with the rules of the game of discord and resolution that Charlie Parker's modernism caused such an uproar in the first place.

There are those who, conscious of their own lack of academic musical knowledge, defend their own opinions about jazz music with a claim on behalf of their own ears, that they can distinguish a felicitous resolution from a fumbling mess although they may not be able to give the technical names of the solecisms. They then dismiss the bulk of modern jazz on the grounds that their ears find it ugly or unintelligible and seem to think there is no more to be said on the subject.

Now the ironic thing is that it is impossible to explain to such people why their technical ignorance is fatal without resorting to the technicalities themselves. The issue is further complicated by the fact that there is a great deal of truth in what they say, if it is applied to the jazz before Parker. In other words, the test they apply to the jazz they don't like is valid only when it is applied to the jazz they do like.

This strikes many people as special pleading because of the implicit assumption that there is a fundamental cleavage between pre- and post-Parker jazz. If the unschooled ear can take in its stride the advance from King Oliver to Louis Armstrong and from Louis Armstrong to Roy Eldridge, which it usually can, why then should it not be able to progress just as happily from Roy Eldridge to Dizzy Gillespie and Fats Navarro? And this is where the first of the technicalities rears its ugly head. Musical harmony and melody may be diatonic or it may be chromatic, and, broadly speaking, the difference between the first forty years of jazz history and the last twenty is that the first was diatonic and the second chromatic.

Why should the layman be able to digest and appreciate diatonic movement and be nonplussed by chromatic movement? Surely it is not good enough just to say that chromaticism is more complex than diatonic thought. After all, Eldridge was more complex harmonically than Armstrong but still presented no real difficulties to the unbigoted ear. The reason is that the difference is not so much one of degree as one of kind. With its advance into the world of chromaticism jazz moved once and for all into the realm of a specialized art form whose understanding and evaluation required specialist knowledge.

The world we live in is a diatonic world. The Western ear is born to a predilection for diatonic scales, diatonic note groupings, diatonic resolution. The hymns we sing are diatonic. The vast bulk of the popular music pouring into our ears from the day we are born is diatonic. When we whistle or sing we whistle or sing diatonically, and although we may not know, when we reach the final cadence of our own casual musical performances, in the bath or walking along the street, that we are moving from the dominant seventh chord to the tonic chord, we will know instantly if someone else makes that movement in some other way. The alien notes will jar on our diatonic ears, and we will claim that somewhere there are wrong notes. By the very nature of our prevailing every-day environment, we are all educated in all the technicalities of music except the actual names of the terms.

The question which often arises at this point is, if diatonic music is so acceptable to our ears, why on earth should musicians want to resort to something else? The question answers itself. The sound which is commonplace to a layman, is going to sound maddeningly tedious to a musician who has to live with the sounds he is making. It will be only a matter of time before the instrumentalist feels limited by working inside a diatonic frame, and begins to explore further afield.

By 1940, the moment when jazz was poised on the brink of its flight into chromaticism, nothing seemed less likely than that very soon there would be a change of direction to transform the face of jazz. The music of the day was tired exhausted, a little disenchanted with itself. This is not to say that every jazz musician was tired, exhausted, disenchanted with himself, or that none of the jazz of the time was worth listening to. Most of the outstanding instrumentalists of the 1930s were still playing, their powers undimmed. Young and Hawkins produced some of their most integrated work after 1940. Charlie Christian never even saw the inside of a recording studio till 1941. It would be cataloguing to extend the list any further.

But the music was tired to the extent that most of it was wholly predictable, always an unhealthy situation in any form of art. Jazz was predictable because the vocabulary of its soloists was more or less the same as it had been for the past ten years. The only extensions had been made by Lester Young, but even these had been founded on a venerable harmonic base. Indeed, it was the very fact that Lester was able to create fresh patterns out of stale raw material which made him so tremendous a figure in the jazz world of the time.

162

There were two main reasons for an event like the arrival of Charlie Parker, apart of course from the truism that it is always in the nature of the young artist to extend his boundaries to the limits of his ability. First, jazz had been stuck long enough in the same diatonic groove for its men to have become hampered by restrictions of harmonic thought. A bright fellow could digest all the laws of the time in a few weeks, although it might take him the rest of his life to make practical instrumental use of his knowledge. G7 still resolved on to C Major or C Minor, no matter whether you were Coleman Hawkins or the second tenor saxophone at the local palais. The path was so well-beaten that it had slowly degenerated into a rut. The other reason was just as understandable. The young rising musician looked around him and was daunted by the stature of the giants of the Swing Age. He was shrewd enough to know there was no sense in attempting an improvement on the styles of Hodges, Carter, Eldridge, Hawkins, for the good reason that these men had invented their own styles. The choice before the apprentice of 1940 was either to become a minor imitator or a revolutionary.

The difficulty is that the revolutionary, if he has no alternative of his own to the *status quo* he is challenging, becomes a mere roughneck. Vital though it was for jazz to find a new approach if it were not to curl up and die from sheer lack of inspiration, at the time, nobody had the faintest glimmering of an idea what the new approach was likely to be, whether it would be instrumental, as Artie Shaw evidently hoped when he toyed with strings and harpsichords, overlooking the fact that a platitude on the piano remains a platitude when it is played on a harpsichord or a spinet or a celeste; or whether the new direction might take the form of a more intense stylization of older conventions, as the Benny Goodman Sextet attempted.

The breakthrough had to come from a young man not yet

163

set in his musical ways. And whoever this young man was to be, he would have to have an ear instinctively attuned to harmonic movement of the most complex kind. He would also have to possess a melodic gift and a sense of form at least as great as any other jazz musician who ever lived, and perhaps greater, for reasons which we will see.

The most daunting condition for this new approach to improvisation was that tradition had apparently to be ignored; I say apparently because in actual fact Charlie Parker's jazz went closer to the roots of the matter than any musician since Louis Armstrong, but for many years the strangeness of the world he created obscured this fact. All kinds of conventions would have to be ignored, not only those of discord and resolution. The old idea of a musicianly tone might have to be ditched, and so might the old idea about the finished performance being immaculate and un-blemished, as Hodges and Carter were. The element of gambling would re-enter the process of making jazz, because the artist would once more be casting himself on an unknown tide.

The peculiar properties of the human ear now enter the argument to cause hopeless confusion. It is one of the physiological features of our species that the most outrageous cacophony might well come to sound perfectly innocuous if only we give it time. Amazing but true, that what sounds like an outrageous gaffe to one generation will be accepted with a yawn by the next. At the time Charlie Parker made his recording début, all but a few musicians and one or two shrewd *afficionados* dismissed him as a buffoon, because to them the progressions he was using seemed grammatically incorrect. And so they were if you judged them according to the method of Johnny Hodges.

The surprising thing is that only a knife-edge separated the one from the other, a fact most conveniently demonstrated by one of the earliest Parker recordings. On the first, subsequently rejected take of 'Red Cross', Parker, coping with the harmonies of 'I Got Rhythm', makes an almost staid start, perhaps because he was on the horns of the same dilemma as the guitarist Tiny Grimes had been when he composed the piece. The first four bars of 'Red Cross' consist of a two-bar repeated phrase suffering from all the ennui of the period. It might have been lifted straight out of one of Benny Goodman's prim little pieces for the sextet. There is not the slightest sign that this is the dawn of a new era in jazz. But then, without any preparation, occurs in the fifth and sixth bars a new-minted phrase which has nothing to do with the phrase that went before. The two fragments belong to different stages of jazz development, and the impact on first hearing is most disturbing. The strange beauty of the new shape is then accented even further by the fact that the two-bar cadence following is as conventional as the opening four bars. It is a bebop sandwich, with the Swing Age playing the part of the bread.

When Parker enters after the theme statement on the first take, his phrase pays such deference to the jazz tradition that it might literally be Johnny Hodges playing something like 'Squatty Roo'. The phrase consists of four notes based harmonically on the tonic major chord. No revolution here, although after this opening the solo careers off on its own strange path. This take was rejected and another immediately cut, and it is now that an apparently minute alteration occurs in the shaping of the first alto phrase, an alteration symbolic of much of the fuss which arose about Parker and what he was about to do to jazz over the next few years.

The first three notes of the four-note entry phrase are identical, almost as though the soloist had made a mental note to play them no matter how many takes there might be. But the last quaver of the phrase flies off in a completely

unexpected direction. The listener hearing it for the first
time is caught flat-footed and can only tell himself that the
man is mad, that he is playing wrong notes in the most
shameless manner, that jazz is nothing like as trustworthy as
it used to be in the good old days. At the time 'Red Cross'
was made, in September 1944, people could get really nasty
with each other over the legitimacy of that fourth note. They
might develop an enmity expressing itself in physical assault,
or if they were musicians, ripen into a vendetta whose
bitterness would remain undiluted for ten or fifteen years.

For all that, there was nothing blasphemous or technically
incorrect about that note, or many others like it that Parker
scattered all over his recordings. It was perfectly permissible.
The only point was that from now on the world of sound
embodied by the term 'jazz' became irrevocably divided into
two factions, those who could accept that note and those who
could not. The question was perhaps a little more complicated than that for many people. There were those willing,
not only to accept that note, but to accept that note and
nothing else, and even to construct around it a philosophy
of social insurrection. They were the crackpots and the professional hipsters who seemed to think that now Charlie
Parker had arrived, everything played before him was placed
out of court. Every extraneous factor about him, from his
dress to his private habits, became an essential part of the
wooing of the new muse.

Acceptance or rejection of that note, and the nature and
degree of the acceptance and rejection of that note, was a kind
of litmus test for the sensitivity of the ear of the judge. Whatever anyone may have felt personally about Charlie Parker
in those days, it was certainly true that very many people who
had regarded themselves, quite sincerely, as jazzlovers, now
found themselves jazzhaters. Some of them were too bewildered about the upheaval to do very much about it, so

they retired in a state of bitterness and complete bewilderment. Some of them, the more spirited ones, tried to concoct the most comical sophistries to retain their position. M. Pannassie made an inspired attempt at defending the castle by claiming that anything he didn't like wasn't jazz at all. Of course he did not say this in so many words, but what he did say was that Charlie Parker's music, or Bebop as it was known in those quaintly onomatopoeic days, was not jazz at all, but some ghastly hybrid which M. Pannassie was very careful not to define.

In other words, a few uses of that note from 'Red Cross' and Charlie Parker had lopped away a huge percentage of jazz followers from the body of the music itself. All the romantics of the 'Red light district of Storyville and Louis in the Reformatory' school were out. All the followers of the New Orleans legend abandoned their position with indecent haste and became self-confessed nostalgia-mongers with no real interest in the present or the future of jazz. All the adulators of the Big Band ethos, with its attendant imbecilities of screaming solos and half-witted novelty, disappeared from view. The trouble was that none of those who objected to that note were really sure of themselves. Not knowing what the note was, or what its syntactical justification might be, or whether it was a joke in poor taste, the anti-Parkerites, or if you like the ante-Parkerites, either gnashed their teeth in ineffectual rage, thus becoming a constant source of amusement to younger musicians, or took the bit between their teeth and entered the lists with the most astonishing theories.

The delicious thing is that the diehards included many musicians who had themselves once been adventurers. Benny Goodman, who evidently believed that now he had stopped evolving himself, everyone else ought to stop evolving too, mumbled something about 'wrong notes'. Louis Armstrong felt so strongly about it that he actually was moved to make a definite statement about music. The beboppers, he remarked, were killing the business. Of course such asperities became diluted with the passing years. Goodman even went so far as to hire Wardell Gray, and Louis Armstrong, perhaps reassured by the fact that business, despite the beboppers, had never been better, was rumoured to be on friendly terms with Dizzy Gillespie of all people. But it is the immediate impact of the new jazz and the lunacies of bigotry and partisanship it caused that is symptomatic of the heresy of Charlie Parker's music.

After reflecting on the magnitude of the dialectical war which raged over the birth of modern jazz, it is ironic to note how innocuous those outrageous notes really were. To slide for a moment into the degeneracy of technicalities once more, the Hodges-like phrase in the first take of 'Red Cross' ended on C, the root of the tonic major chord, whereas in the second take the phrase ended on a movement from F sharp to F natural, and the F sharp was none other than that dreaded scourge of the reactionaries, the terror of the sentimentalists, the bane of the professional fans, the pretenders and the usurpers, the Flattened Fifth.

Now the flattened fifth of the common chord is not right and it is not wrong, in the same way that when a man accepts as silence what a dog will bark at as a piercing scream, neither the man nor the dog is right or wrong. It is simply a question of the relative sensitivity of their ears. To a man whose musical experience is limited to listening to jazz, and jazz of the past at that, the flattened fifth will indeed sound like a mocking insult. On the other hand, the musician who has heard even a few bars of the Impressionist composers, the same ones who captivated the young Bix Beiderbecke, cannot honestly see what all the fuss is about. With Charlie Parker jazz was simply trying to catch up with the movement of formal music into the realms of chromaticism which had swept across the entire world of music during the nineteenth century. It is no coincidence that the composers whom adventurous jazzmen always prefer are Debussy, Ravel, Stravinsky and Bartok, and that they, who too have their bigoted moments, cannot often tolerate more than a few bars of a composer like Handel, who probably represents to them the classical counterpart of a mouldy fig.

What the modern movement was doing was to broaden the harmonic territory available to the improvising musician, which brings us to the Olympian achievement of Charlie Parker. The more complex the harmony, the more difficult becomes the soloist's task of retaining the relaxed spirit of a good jazz performance. Once a tune begins, the harmonic changes rush by like telegraph poles on a railway line, and the more poles there are the harder it becomes to pay full attention to them all, until in the end so preoccupied with them will the traveller become that he is in real danger of failing to observe the unity of the surrounding landscape. Parker was so richly endowed a musician that he was not only able to introduce into the jazz context shades of harmonic subtlety never before heard in jazz, but he was able at the same time to restore to jazz an emotional sincerity it had forgotten about in the preceding era of sophisticated techniques, ambitious orchestrations, and compromise with the tastes of the dance hall.

The two effects are apparently contradictory. How can a man complicate an art form technically and at the same time simplify it emotionally? He can only achieve this if his emotional depth is so profound that not only can it cleanse the existing form with its attendant rules and conventions, but can accept further complexities and still manage to retain the effect of simplicity. That is why Charlie Parker might be said to have possessed a melodic gift greater than any other

169

jazz musician before him. The mere fact of his success proves the point. Had he not possessed a prodigious instinct for the moulding of a clean and beautiful phrase, his work would have been doomed to the same arid precosity of many of his contemporaries and followers, who were too often guilty of a kind of instrumental chicane, by which the passion of inspiration is usurped by an impressive but fundamentally pointless manual dexterity.

At first Parker was not able to produce the thoroughly integrated performance in the new idiom, because jazz happens to be a communal effort. No matter how great he may have been, Parker was not able to conjure up rhythm sections to complement his own playing. In recordings like 'Red Cross' can be found the intriguing and slightly comic spectacle of the new jazz presented against the old familiar background of four chunks to a bar. Only in time did a comprehensive world of modernism come into being.

What must have surprised the old guard of the jazz world, players and spectators alike, was Parker's repeated insistence on the twelve bar blues, a form which although it had not gone into complete decline, had not been too happily used by the outstanding musicians of the Swing Age. The reason is not hard to find. Players like Hawkins and Carter required for the fulfilment of their styles, sophisticated and ornate, material whose harmonies were far more complex than the blues, with its three indispensable harmonic changes. As it never occurred to these players to take the blues form and amend it, the only alternative was to borrow themes like 'Body and Soul' or 'Out of Nowhere' from the popular song idiom, because these tunes had ever-moving harmonies designed by trained musicians in original patterns.

But Parker had superior endowment to his predecessors, talented as they were. He was more conversant than they with unusual harmonic shapes, and in addition, had a creative spark which was not quite the same as that which enables the soloist to play a succession of good jazz choruses. Parker's ear instinctively heard harmonies implied in a melody which most musicians never thought about. He was therefore tempted to insert into his harmonic sequences chords that were not wrong, but different from those originally written into the song. These new harmonies, or 'substitutions', as some musicians refer to them, are the key to his whole aesthetic. If the jazz soloist is an artist who creates his effect by weaving designs in the harmonies of a theme, then it is quite obvious that when those harmonies are strangely fresh, then the patterns comprising his solos will themselves be strangely fresh, although only if the instrumentalist involved is a gifted jazz musician will the patterns be more than just unusual. There were dozens of early modernists who produced strange patterns, but Parker's strangeness was profound and beautiful. In using the blues form, he was making it most embarrassing for the diehards whose ears were unable to guide them through the labyrinth of Parker's musical thought.

Some of the most superlative Parker recordings are those of the blues, and now that the captains and the kings have departed, nobody, not even the most crackpotted bigot, denies their virtues, for he knows that time has reversed the situation, that it is now he, not the recordings, that are on trial. Even so, allowing for all the belated wisdom of hindsight, it is hard to accept the fact that bloody critical battles raged about such recordings as 'Now's the Time', which in retrospect is seen to be one of the classic blues recordings in the entire jazz repertoire.

Parker plays three choruses on the issued master of 'Now's the Time', and although there are some dazzling innovations, it is very simple to chart the parallel between this interpretation of the blues and any of a thousand from earlier stages in jazz development. Parker's entrance, for instance. There is nothing at all revolutionary about this beautifully conceived, perfectly executed and meticulously defined phrase. It was original certainly, but there was nothing revolutionary about it. It happens to have been played by a revolutionary, but that is not the same thing. Its strangeness was due, not to its harmonic inspiration, of which there is virtually none, but to the breathtaking freshness of the player's style, as though he had heard about the common chord of the major triad for the first time a few minutes before the recording began. These simple, passionate phrases were to remain one of the staples of Parker's style, an antidote he employed instinctively to balance the complexity of some of his bewildering flights into double tempo.

After the first four bars, moving into the minor tonality, the phrase is once again quite simple, although not so stark as the opening. In this second section of the first chorus, there occur at least two intimations of a very important truth about jazz, which is that each new style demands its own technique, because each new style is only new at all because it moves through the harmonies over a path not previously exploited. Parker's phrase is built around the device of a fall from the keynote to the minor third, but not as Hodges might have executed it. There is no suggestion of a glissando. Instead, the intervening notes are lightly touched, no more than suggested, in the descent. The device is executed so casually that it might go unnoticed. However, for the saxophonist with aspirations to master the new idiom, here was a new problem to be solved. When Parker repeats the phrase another characteristic of what was then called Bebop rears its head. After the second descend the phrase climbs upwards again, but instead of a continuous sweep, there is a quaver followed by a triplet, executed as fast as light, but with every detail perfectly defined. Because it was one of the few tangibles of Parker's personal keyboard style, this triplet device came to be one of the most maddening cliches of modern jazz for several years, reducing more than one individual style to the dimensions of a prolonged and ugly hiccup. To Parker it was only one of many personal quirks of style never allowed to shatter the whole. The third and last four-bar section of his first chorus is conventional, except for the fact that infinitesimal adjustments of the time values of the notes hints at an independence of the four-in-a-bar cage which had hitherto been sedulously avoided in jazz.

The second chorus opens with a modest elaboration of the start of the previous chorus, except that at the end of the second bar the appearance, brief but significant, of the augmented second of the key implies one of the substituted chords which gave Parker's playing a new dimension of beauty. It is important to appreciate that this note was the augmented second and not the minor third. In their actual pitch the two notes are the same, but the enharmonic distinction must be made to underline the nature of the harmony in whose terms Parker was thinking. The first real shock to the Establishment comes in the second section, where the melody makes a sudden astonishing leap upwards to create an interval so perplexing to the jazz ear of the time that some people assumed that the high note in the phrase was a slip of the fingers not intended by the soloist at all.

Having flown off at a tangent in this way, Parker then proceeds to another convention of the new jazz, the deployment of an extended passage in double time. It should be made clear that playing sixteen notes in a bar was nothing new. What made these phrases sound like a lunatic scramble to the ear too sluggish to follow them was not the mere presence of the sixteen notes in one bar, but the arrangement of the inflexions and time values to suggest that for a moment or two the tempo of the performance had actually doubled. The effect of this on the listener of the time was catastrophic, for he now had not only to digest new modes of expression, but to digest them at exactly twice the speed for which his mind had been prepared at the start of the performance.No wonder so many people gave up in disgust, overlooking the fact that the melodic content of a phrase like the one which ended the second of Parker's choruses in 'Now's the Time' was ravishing.

The third chorus begins with yet another variation of the phrase that opened the alto solo, only now there are to be found sprinkled about the phrases certain grace notes embellishing the melodic line and seem to complicate it without actually doing so. These grace notes were another Parker mannerism that broke out in an unsightly rash of affectation right across the face of modern jazz, but here again Parker himself kept this kind of virtuosity strictly in check, subordinating its effect to the overall welfare of the solo.

As he approaches the third and final cadence of this last chorus, the soloist breaks out again in a passionate outburst of double-tempo phrasing. It is when he arrives at one of the key junctures of the blues sequence, the eighth bar, that he coins an epigram as beautifully rounded as any that jazz had heard. The eighth bar of the blues is vital because it is one of the moments of resolution at which the soloist arrives on his way round the harmonic cycle, back to the starting tonality, the point where the mood recedes to the quietism of the opening. The harmonic change he uses at the end of the eighth bar is the one that will lead him back to the dominant chord linked to the tonic on which he must end. In modern jazz the ear of many of its pioneers, instead of settling for a normal diatonic change, substituted a tiny progression of descending minor seventh chords. It must not be thought that players like Charlie Parker suddenly discovered a new musical effect. The chord of the minor seventh is as old as music itself. Ravel's 'Allegro for Harp', written before Parker was born, opens with an elaborate exposition of the use of the progression, but the descending minor seventh was not the kind of discord on which the mind of a musician might settle unless he were quite free of the conventions of diatonic harmony.

In effect, Parker, in using these descending minor sevenths, was in the enviable position of having at his disposal a musical device virtually unknown to the idiom in which he was working. Suggestions of the movement may be found in jazz of an earlier period. There is one moment on 'Billie's Blues', recorded in 1937, when Bunny Berigan of all people, seems about to stumble on the sequence. But with Parker it is clear that the effect is designed, intended, thoroughly digested and integrated into the framework of the most traditional of all jazz forms. The phrase Parker coins is romantically overwhelming. Its technical originality is secondary. It is the emerging melodic shape that is vital, and it is at such moments that Parker demonstrates this astonishing gift for bequeathing to future generations of jazz musicians a new harmonic scope at the same time as he cuts away all the fripperies and false sophistications, leaving a residue which, for all its technical ingenuity, is emotionally simple and frank. It is in its complete candour that Parker's style is something new in jazz music. With phrases like his entrance in 'Now's the Time', and the minor seventh device later in the same recording, he bridges the vast gulf between audience and performer through the alchemy of an almost desperate sincerity.

In the sense that he was a sublimely gifted jazz musician, Parker was something of a freak. Never at any time could the listener, no matter how well acquainted with Parker's playing he might be, feel confident that Parker would not play something unexpected. Of course he had his private cliches. All musicians do. They are the means by which we identify them. There were times when Parker might jog along, putting

175

a solo together with no more than a high degree of professionalism without venturing beyond the familiar limits of his own more casual performances. But he was always able suddenly to rise above himself to produce yet another solo unique in form and scope. One of the most enlightening demonstrations of Parker's creative muse at work has been preserved in the London Memorial album which includes several different masters of the blues theme, 'Billie's Bounce'.

The first four takes are frankly routine Parker, comprising phrases a little too familiar because of the enlightening effect Parker has had upon the jazz world in the years since he made these early blues records. Not till the fifth take did he arrive at the synthesis he was seeking. In this final acceptable version of 'Billie's Bounce' the actual structure of the phrases is not so very different from that of the first four, although in the opening phrase of the fourth chorus he suddenly takes us off through a strangely beautiful little byway on the way to the dominant chord of the key which nobody had thought of before. It is in the moulding of the phrases and their relevance to each other that the ultimate solo has a perfection the first four lack. The phrases now blend into a single entity, transforming four choruses of the blues into one extended statement. The solo is no longer explicable in technical terms because its virtues are now more than technical.

Once again the first chorus opens with conventional use of the blues harmonies. At the end of the second four-bar section the last two notes, technically elementary, merely the major seventh and major sixth of the key, achieve a truly extraordinary pathos, suggesting the overtones of a verbal statement of warmth and candour now well-known to those familiar with Parker's playing. The second chorus opens with a sudden terrifying independence of the bar lines. For a bar or two the whole of jazz seems to be reeling crazily away from the discipline of tempo. Chaos is imminent until in the second two bars of the first four-bar block, Parker restores the conventional pulse of a jazz performance with a metrical little phrase that jumps back on the tramlines. It is a fleeting moment bursting with implications. There is no way in which it can be notated because the microscopic adjustments of the time values cannot be expressed in terms of crotchets and quavers. For those few brief beats the rhythmic formalism of jazz is left to fend for itself while the soloist appears to wander off on some rhythmic plane of his own. Were it not for the irresistible authority of the phrase in the third and fourth bars, pulling the solo back to its metrical obligations as a performance in the jazz frame, one might be tempted to believe that Parker's mind had wandered for a moment and was concentrating on some private musical experience of his own of which nobody else was aware. The chorus ends with one of those fervent double-tempo outbursts, which, so far from being expositions of technical expertise, are vital to the solo because only through their agency does the soloist feel able to express all the pent-up jazz inside him bursting to be free.

The third chorus begins with another return to the simplicity of a first-year primer. The phrase is no more than the unadorned arpeggio of the tonic chord, but it does not sound simpletonian because of its place in a pattern of considerable complexity. The phrase persists longer than the listener is led to expect. Instead of the open space in the second half of the phrase apparently implied by the contours of the first half, the notes come tumbling out until the whole of the first four bars are filled out by one long phrase of rare extended ingenuity. The solo then closes on a more or less traditional flourish.

In both 'Now's the Time' and 'Billies Blues', two of the most mature blues performances ever recorded, our retrospective wisdom tells us of the surprisingly high content of purely conventional harmonic vocabulary in Parker's playing. The revolution seen through the window of 'Billie's Bounce' appears to have been a far milder affair than the warring factions of the 1940s believed it to be. Above all else is revealed the reckless confusion and bigotry of those intolerable fatheads who screamed that Charlie Parker was not playing jazz. 'Now's the Time' and 'Billie's Bounce' are jazz in its purest, most concentrated form. M. Pannassie, an unrepentant clutcher at straws ever since modernism first appeared, has shown a tedious persistence in making capital out of a quotation of Parker's stating that 'bebop was no love-child of jazz', as though the casual remark of an artist in the midst of his labours is necessarily of relevance to the nature of his art.

The comical thing is that M. Pannassie has insisted on an interpretation of the statement that suits his own ends, which are frankly so incomprehensible that one loses sight of them. It seems far more probable to me that what Parker meant if and when he said that bebop was no love-child of jazz, was that there are no grounds on which anybody could challenge the legitimacy of the succession from 'Wild Man Blues' to 'Sippin' at Bells'.

For all that legitimacy, modern jazz in its early days found itself in desperate straits. Not only did the bulk of the jazz audience find its offerings indigestible, but many of the musicians of the preceding era rejected it just as uncompromisingly, although no doubt in some cases for very different reasons. The practising jazz musician with a set style will always have a vested interest in the *status quo*. Many of the anti-Parker musicians must have felt the ground slipping under their feet when first they heard the strains of 'Thriving from a Riff'. One of the most pathetic spectacles in all jazz history is that of the modernists twisting and turning to find some way out of the impasse of their own forbidding complexity without sacrificing anything in artistic content. The means they employed varied from slapstick and buffoonery, symbolized in Dizzy Gillespie's comic hats, to the courting of those trappings of musical legitimacy jazz has always coveted. It has occurred to many people that there might have been something regrettable in the wedding of an uninhibited musician like Charlie Parker to the cosseted sound of a string section. To some the 'Parker with Strings' sessions were as unforgivable as Bix's spell with Paul Whiteman. To others, it was a momentary aberration on Parker's part that left his gift unblemished. It has occurred to very few commentators that Parker himself may have been delighted by the experiment of soaring high over a landscape of stringed instruments.

Instrumental virtuosity reached a new climax with Charlie Parker. All previous laws were invalid. Collective improvisation in the light of a Parker performance like 'Embraceable You' was now clearly seen to be a compensatory device to cloak the limitations of the musicians who resorted to it. With a musician of Parker's genius, the solo voice was the only conceivable approach, because it was the only way he would be able to suggest to the listener more than a tithe of his potential. The string background was still no more than a background and had no bearing on the actual content of the saxophone solos. Had Parker been distressed or thrown out of his stride by the experiment then the decriers would have been justified. In fact, both on his own testimony and that of the records, Parker thoroughly enjoyed the whole affair.

The 'Parker with Strings' tracks are another demonstration of the soloist's refusal to be disconcerted and therefore inhibited by the intensity of his own passion. Performances like 'Just Friends' and 'If I Should Lose You' are towering examples of musical romanticism. They are unashamedly sentimental without ever degenerating into mere sentimentality, and they also exhibit one facet of Parker's sublimity which was accepted for many years, and is indeed often challenged today. He had one of the most inexpressively beautiful instrumental tones any jazzman ever produced. Because it was not the dandiacal, elegant tone of Benny Carter or the voluptuous cry of Johnny Hodges, it was dismissed as a fraud by critics who had never blown any instruments in their lives, apart possibly from their own trumpets. Bandleaders hated it, and still do in Britain, because it wrought havoc with the vibrato blend of the conventional saxophone section. And purists complained that more than one Parker recording was issued although blemished by the indiscretion of a squeak.

It was true that Parker sounded like neither Hodges nor Carter. It was also true that he sounded more inspired than either of them. The laws of saxophone section playing may be discounted, for they were formulated for the edification of dance hall patrons and have no musical significance. As for the squeaks, they were the occasional price Parker had to pay for the power he produced from an alto saxophone. Now and again he put into his embouchure more muscular pressure than any reed or mouthpiece could cope with, hence the squeak. Sometimes the squeaks caused a recording to be rejected, but in certain cases the solo was so outstanding that the master was released, squeak and all, just as a publishing firm might elect to release on to the market a great literary masterpiece with a small print smudge on every hundredth page.

What is more to the point is that when a saxophonist squeaks it is no reflection on his musicianship. It may imply a condemnation of his reed, his mouthpiece or his selection of these two appurtenances, but it has literally nothing to do with his technical ability. There are thousands of saxophonists who never squeaked in their lives, but this does not place them above Charlie Parker in the hierarchy of jazz. The modern revolution was a hectic affair. Its pioneers had no time for the niceties of public performance.

Parker was an experimenter, an explorer, forever poised on the brink of chaos, just as some of those he displaced as the pre-eminent jazz voice had been poised for ten years or more on the brink of latitude. He was attempting to hammer out a whole set of conventions new to jazz, and considering the complete originality of his playing, it is truly miraculous that he achieved as many perfect performances as he did.

With Parker, jazz was rising phoenixlike from the debris of its own ashes. It was being given another chance. Parker was bestowing upon it a mine of musical thought so rich in potential that his successors have been quarrying the mine ever since. Unlike Parker, most of these successors are not unlimited jazz soloists, finding it an indispensable aid to inspiration to lean on the teachings of Parker. They are also on occasions hamstrung by musical climates that Parker was able to take in his stride. Big band, small band, strings or trumpet-alto front line, vocal groups, scat singers, nothing impeded the flow of his expression.

Some of the big band sides he made in the middle 1950s are thrilling matches between the orchestra on one hand and Parker on the other. The orchestrations are ordinary enough, and time has been particularly harsh on them, but Parker redeems all. Time and again he soars over the concerted voice of the accompaniment, painting dazzling resplendent pictures which take the breath away. The infinite grace of his variations on 'Stella by Starlight', the whimsical chromatic tricks he plays with the first phrase of 'What is This Thing Called Love?', that hair-raising moment when he soars over the written melody by a mere semitone in 'Almost Like Being In Love' so that the ear is almost too terrified to follow,

181

all these manifestations of the soloist's genius make otherwise indifferent recordings historic.

When a man towers over the whole realm of his artistic exploits, it is certain that for some time after he has gone, critical standards will be all awry, like a trusty compass sudden fallen inside the field of a mightly magnet. Parker's recognition, like Lester's, was belated, with the difference that while Lester lived to see the vindication of his methods, Parker did not. The pathos of the situation is increased by the fact that Parker missed out only by a year or two. Had he lived into the 1960s he would have been lionized as Gillespie was lionized, he would have become at forty the Grand Old Man of a glorious artistic triumphal upheaval. He would even have made large sums of money, something always pleasing to jazz musicians, no matter what any of them may say to the contrary. But he did not live. He actively strove to die, for personal reasons which nobody can adequately explain. It is too glib to say he became a drug addict for the same reason Alice ate the cake marked 'Eat Me', to gain entry into the enchanted garden. And no less glib to say he behaved as he did because of his confrontation by the long line of blank uncomprehending faces which for years showed no reaction to the music he was conjuring up out of his own head. What terrifying private visions might have dogged him, what oppression might have fell upon him through his inescapable artistic loneliness, what disgust he might have succumbed to when the imbecile denigrations poured in, we do not know. His life was a turbulent enigma and the only coherence to emerge from it was the music.

During a career short even by jazz standards, he wrecked the canons of criticism and severed the music for ever from the dilettante followers to whom an affectation of jazz enthusiasm was a social asset or a personal vanity. After Parker you had to be something of a musician to follow the best jazz of the day. If you were sentimental about the good old days, if you clutched at fading recollections of your own adolescence, if you thought your opinions were valid just because you possessed the recordings, Parker exposed you for a charlatan. There was nothing left for you to do but feign wisdom of his art, like the professional hipsters and the beat writers, or run screaming from the arena, like the revivalists and those who collected matrix numbers as a schoolboy collects train numbers, without wit or selectivity.

Even if you were conversant with the grammar and syntax of the language Parker was using, it was improbable that you would be able to grasp the full import of what he was pioneering. It is a sad reflection of jazz development since Parker that what we call modernism is already twenty years old, that what Charlie Parker played in the early 1940s still has about it a contemporary ring carrying a damning implied criticism of those who have followed him. Any of a hundred Parker recordings prove the point, for all of them contain the raw material for a thousand solos recorded by others in later years. The phrases still sound fresh today, yet they were routine to Parker years ago, thrown off by him in the course of his life as a working musician as casually as another musician might race through a few warming-up exercises.

The extent to which he was passed over by professed experts is truly extraordinary. What of the earless ones who said he was playing wrong notes? What of those brilliant analysts who announced the whole thing was a practical joke? What of those who denied his music the descriptive adjective 'jazz'? There was one priceless philistine who took his tape recorder to the Mintons sessions and switched off whenever Parker started to play, because his jazz was not as decorous as that of Herbie Fields, a musician whom the owner of the machine worshipped to such an insane degree that he compiled tape after tape.

When Parker went to Sweden in 1950 the conditions were the worst possible from the point of view of the preservation of the incident. There was only a tape recorder of inadequate technical potential, and a rhythm section not fit to wipe Parker's boots. He shared the front line with a trumpeter who was no more than a competent professional, certainly a soloist lacking in the inventive flair of any of the important soloists of the modern era. As always, Parker was sublimely indifferent to these limitations, in rather the same way that Bix was to the solecisms of the lesser Chicagoans. Parker's visit to Sweden took place in 1950, yet the content of his solos on that occasion were providing raw material for outstanding saxophonists ten years later. Because of the crude recording conditions, much of the passionate warmth of his tone is lost, but the unflagging imagination makes the evening an important one. The incongruity of the background, an incongruity musical as well as regional, simply did not affect his music at all.

Some years after his death it was still possible to pass muster as a modernist in the London jazz clubs by repeating, a semitone higher, a phrase just played on the tonic chord. In the Swedish album, Parker resorts to this device in the opening bars of the second eight of his third improvised chorus of 'Anthropology', pursuing what must have been for the times a highly subjective harmonic logic of his own, one it needed considerable artistic courage to follow. It is difficult to say whether the Swedish rhythm section hung on to his coat-tails at moments like this, because the recording balance is so poor that it may well be concealing a multitude of musical sins.

In 'Cheers', one of the earliest standard themes of the modern revolution, at the end of the first eight of his second chorus, Parker races down the chord of the diminished seventh, placing grace notes before each note of the chord, a facet of his virtuosity which Stan Getz later indulged in on every possible occasion, no doubt finding the device peculiarly suited to the rococo embellishments of his own highly florid style. To point the mastery of Parker over his material and the circumstances under which he sometimes had to treat it, there is the presence on the other side of the record of the Swedish alto saxophonist Arne Domnerus, whose jazz in contrast to Parker's sounds circumspect, not quite sure of itself, and therefore premeditated, as though Domnerus believed that the freedom Parker had bequeathed to the jazz soloist was too vast an affair for the intuitive muse to cope with. This generosity of spirit of Parker's is the true hallmark of his quality. The limitless chromatic freedom of his new jazz was like the armour of Achilles, there for anybody to try on for size whenever he felt like it, but too much for many to cope with.

Earlier in the same year Parker had fulfilled another ballroom date which was taped and later issued as an authentic album. The 'Bird at St Nick's' issue is a better production in every way than the transcription of the evening in the Amiralen Ballroom in Malmo. The instrumental balance is better, and the other musicians have a sensitive appreciation of the kind of music Parker was trying to produce. For reasons of economy the tracks were trimmed up into excerpts that spotlight Parker at the expense of everyone else, but despite this, the 'St Nick's' album has about it an element of truth which many studio recordings do not.

It was one of the first examples we ever had of the modern jazz musician out in the world selling his music to the customers of a dance hall. It is instantly clear what Parker was up against. The broken rhythms and cascades of notes which might seem, to the uneducated ear, to wreak havoc with the tempo, the splendour of the saxophonist's whole conception, none of these things are ever likely to commend themselves to patrons raised on and looking for the conventional dance hall pap. In fact, there is a schism here that no amount of striving on the artist's part can ever hope to resolve. This is the fundamental difference between Parker's music and the jazz of all the preceding generations. With Parker jazz had evolved to the stage where it was too complex to be accepted merely as a background for that Saturday night social round of the dancer. It was now ceasing to be a functional music in so far as the only way to arrive at any depth of understanding was not to dance to it, or eat with it in the distant background, or discuss abstruse philosophy to the promptings of its rhythms, but to listen to it, intently, respectfully, with all the sensitivity one can muster, because it was a maturing art form demanding full attention or none at all.

In the 'St Nick's' album are all the elements in the life of a jazz musician which create the exquisite irony of his situation. The dancers shuffle round on their treadmill, the extraneous noises of the patrons drift in over the music, the acoustics are distorted by the accidental echo-chamber effect of most indoor arenas. And Parker tries to cut across these factors, playing the most amazing music, jazz fresh-minted, somehow implying a relationship with the early jazz that the Pannassies of this world doggedly refused to see, and yet carrying with it the implications of the era in which it flowered, as unmistakably as the Bix records re-echo the Roaring Twenties and Goodman's soporifics with the big band are characteristic of the college tastes of the New Deal.

What does a musician do in this unfortunate situation? Does he fret at the thought of his art being misused? Does he attempt to make converts? At first he might possibly attempt to do both these things, but as he slowly becomes worldly-wise, he does the only thing left to him. He ignores all the extraneous factors as completely as possible. He shuts his mind off from the imbecilities of his audiences. He throws his music at the heads of whoever happen to be within earshot. As far as he is concerned, the audience happens to be there by accident. It is he, and not they, who is the focal point of the event. The fact that their admission fee is paying his wage for the night would only have some bearing on the artist-and-audience relationship if with their admission fee they contributed a guarantee of sensitivity, of willingness to understand, of awareness. But most audiences do not, especially in dance halls, and it is perfectly clear that in the 'Bird at St Nick's' album Parker and the rest of them are just going through the motions of earning a living. Somebody has booked them for a gig. They have accepted it gracefully. The creation of a work of art is so alien to their thoughts and attitudes that the suggestion of it would only inspire them to ribaldry. But they have created art, for all their avowed indifference to such a grandiose conception. Parker at St Nick's is earning a living for a single night of his life, but in doing so he is also minting a few gems which may fly over the heads of the shuffling dancers but remain on the record for connoisseurs to prise out of the content if they feel so inclined.

This forsaking of his audience by the modern musician is the most vital and tragic fact in all the evolution of jazz. It was inevitable, because the moment musicians began to explore the possibilities of the world of harmony, instead of accepting without question the narrow conventions of the early days, sounds were imminent which required for their appreciation a comparatively trained ear, the very thing that audiences have never been able to give the jazz musician. There is no solution. Parker was right to dream of subtleties like 'Confirmation' instead of attempting to cut his way through the jungle of ignorance and prejudice to a popular acclaim. When an artist is able to conjure up work of the sublime beauty of the best Parker, it is the duty, not of the artist to reach down to the outside world, but of the outside

187

world to aspire to the heights of the artist, wherein is contained all the elements of Charlie Parker's tragedy.

For it was indeed a tragedy in the classic sense. The end was ordained before the beginning. He was haunted by the incubus of a consummate musical gift all his life. He was no dance band musician, no happy member of the ensemble. He was a lone musical spirit to whom compromise was an alien and uncomprehended thing. The playing speaks without compromise. There is no fooling when Parker plays. He puts into it everything he knows and feels. The best he can hope for is that somehow the emotional force of the performance will convey itself to ears unversed in the laws of harmonic exploration.

In the years since Parker's death, appreciation of his kind of jazz is said to have increased vastly. That is not quite true. The following for jazz has vastly increased, certainly, but it is doubtful whether a true understanding of Charlie Parker's jazz is much more widespread than it was. Today Sonny Stitt and Cannonball Adderley sell better than ever Charlie Parker dared to dream. But the same people who listen to Stitt and discern the springs of passion and musical literacy at the roots of the style, may often come to Parker's recordings at a later date, and wonder what all the fuss was about. The saxophonists who followed Parker built a comprehensive lexicon out of his prolific vocabulary, giving it a superficial polish which helps to span that chasm between artist and audience without making the complexities of the style itself any clearer.

When Stitt tumbles into one of those double-tempo cascades, the listener, sophisticated by his exposure to Stitt's previous records, and in some cases the Parker legacy too, can predict the moment when Stitt will end that flurry of notes and play, almost as though it were ordained by some supernal studio dictator, one of those simple, free, blithe phrases to counterbalance the semi-quavers, lending poise to the form of the solo. Just as most people came to an understanding, at least in part, of Lester Young's style through the agency of Zoot Sims and Stan Getz, so Charlie Parker's music has become a commonplace, a thing to be taken for granted, because of the way in which Stitt, Phil Woods and the other Parker idolators, have understandably capitalized on his originality and rendered it less frightening.

The result is that world from which Parker's music sprang is forgotten and its feats therefore underrated. There can be no conception of what he did, unless one is conversant with the jazz of the early 1940s, just as it is pointless discussing Lester Young without an awareness that Hawkins existed before him. Some of the early Parker recordings are so firmly planted in older roots that it is easy to forget the extent to which his personal style grew out of the Swing Age, a fact that makes his music not less but more remarkable.

As late as December 1945, Parker found himself in musical situations which fundamentally belonged to earlier days in jazz. One of the bitterest episodes of Parker's career was the visit to California, where he, with Lucky Thompson, Milt Jackson, Al Haig, Ray Brown, Stan Levy and Dizzy Gillespie, was booked into Billy Berg's club. It would be enlightening to know what Parker thought of this adventure before he undertook it. Presumably there must have been some optimism about West Coast audiences. In the event, the audiences on Vine Street damned themselves beyond all redemption. They were not indifferent but positively hostile. It would be easy to make out a case for them, that the music was so advanced for its day that its musicians had no right to play it, that the man who pays for a ticket has some say in the performance. But this was a jazz club, and it audiences ought to have been prepared for adventurousness. The ticketbuyer's true function is to sit there and keep his mouth shut and his ears open. This the patrons of Billy Berg's refused to do. Their hostility must have had a deeply depressing effect on a musician so highly-strung as Parker, for whom the incident remained one of the low-water marks of his life.

Before abandoning the West Coast to its own resources, Parker and Gillespie participated in a recording session organized in Los Angeles by Slim Gaillard. All four tracks are based on the simplest of jazz forms, the blues, 'I Got Rhythm' and 'Honeysuckle Rose'. The rhythm section chugs along in the authentic style of the 1930s. Solo time is restricted to the old three-minute limitations of the 78 rpm recording. Parker is here working within the jazz frame he was to wreck beyond repair. The only element of modernism in the performance is indeed the playing of he and Dizzy Gillespie. It is one of the most revealing sessions in which Parker was ever involved, for the two worlds of jazz are here about to part company, the diatonic world to turn in on itself seeking recapitulation of the past, the chromatic world to stride on ahead and take whatever might come.

The upheaval caused by Charlie Parker has not subsided. It has left the critics and some of the musicians shattered in their confidence. Nobody can forget the crass errors of judgment which followed on Parker's arrival. Decriers have hastily recanted and even become pro-modernists. But the results have been curious. An innovator was once slanged, but he turned out to be a great musician. Therefore, says the world of jazz, we must never again slang an innovator. Charlie Parker was a great musician and he was an innovator. Therefore all innovators are great musicians. The syllogism is so false that it sounds like a joke, but it is a very serious thing. The Ornette Colemans of this world are indulged in because of the mistake everyone made over Charlie Parker. Anybody who cannot enjoy Coleman is accused of abysmal reaction. But, in fact, anybody who adopts this cowardly critical attitude is proving once more that he has not the faintest idea what Charlie Parker's arrival was all about. Parker's jazz is built on irrevocable harmonic logic, none the less irrevocable because it happens to be beyond the scope of many people who profess to understand it. The younger modern experimenters, in courting some nebulous lunacy called Free Form, which is really no form at all, are applying the direct negation of Parker's methods. They are abandoning the very harmonic discipline which gave strength and grace to Parker's eloquence. One thing it is safe to say. Parker himself would not be surprised. His career was the final link in the chain of jazz evolution which rendered it an art form. Once any activity becomes an art form, however reluctantly it may have achieved the status, good and bad will disappear. In their place will be substituted critical theories. In the meantime, all the innovations in the world cannot alter the truth that the greatest jazz is that which has melodic grace, harmonic courage and the sense of form which can miraculously render abstract musical improvisation into genuine artistic expression. Jazz today awaits the coming of another Charlie Parker. When he arrives, it will no doubt cast at his head the same brickbats it heaved at Bix Beiderbecke, Lester Young and Charlie Parker. Critical brickbats are apparently just as durable as great jazz records.

7

•••

ART TATUM

In Feather's *Encyclopedia of Jazz*, out of 126 pianists asked to name their prime influence, 78 nominate Art Tatum. Elsewhere in the same volume the editor tells us that in a poll conducted among one hundred of the most famous jazz musicians, 68 placed Tatum first in their list of preferences. In an art form where tastes have always been bafflingly fragmented and judgements bewilderingly contradictory, such comparative unanimity is stupefying. It is as though 78 out of the world's 126 most distinguished novelists were to plump for Proust, or 68 out of the world's one hundred most gifted painters were to agree on Velasquez. Such events could never conceivably happen, and yet in so notoriously fissiparous an area as jazz music, an area renowned for its schools and schisms and cults and pigeonholes, it appears that one man has so dominated his instrument that roughly two out of every three of his professional rivals prefer his mastery to anyone else's, including their own. Of course it might be said that all such manifestations of the democratic process are meaningless when applied to relative merits in the arts, but it is as well to remember that while most jazz polls are conducted either among members of the public, who know little about comparative judgements, or among critics, who know even less, the Tatum polls were held among men who earned their livelihood by the same methods as Tatum did, that is, making music, and that therefore their unanimity is not to be taken lightly.

193

Who was Art Tatum? He was born on October 13, 1910 in Toledo, Ohio, the son of a mechanic who had migrated north from North Carolina. He was born totally blind in one eye and with only slight vision in the other (it is said that he could distinguish some colours and, by holding the cards close to his face, play an efficient game of pinochle), so that of the myriad things he was never able to see, the most significant was a note of music printed on a sheet of paper. The importance of this fact in arriving at some understanding of his style is obviously paramount. It is a truism that many of the great baroque recorded masterpieces in jazz are of a technical complexity which would be quite beyond the ability of their creators to play them were they faced with the notes written out as a composition. But the very essence of jazz, the one element in the mechanics of making it which separates it from all other forms, is the fact that the improvisor, by exploiting the art of impromptu composition, or extemporisation as it used to be called, has short-circuited the creative process in music. The notes go from mind to keyboard without the intervening stage of manuscript, so that by an irony too deep to plumb, the blind musician finds in jazz a world where his handicap is of relatively no consequence and sometimes even an advantage, for to be uncorrupted, as it were, by the sight of music that has congealed into composition, the pianist can evolve an essentially pianistic style based on intimacies of the tactile sense.

And this is where Tatum's style becomes so problematic for the jazz world. He seems to have done all the unorthodox things so far as style and development are concerned. He matured at an absurdly precocious age, for instance, long before other jazz musicians have even found their way around the main roads of the harmonic map. A bass player called June Cole, who once worked with McKinney's Cotton Pickers, claimed to have heard Tatum for the first time at a gambling joint, and said that already the Tatum style was fully formed, the Tatum technique fully controlled. The year of this reminiscence is 1925, which puts Tatum in mid-teens at the very most. Another rare fact about Tatum is that once he arrived he stayed. There was no trial period, no quibbling about his status as a master, no haggling about his acceptance. There were one or two dips in his popularity, but these were only comparative; and must have concerned Tatum as little as they now concern posterity. Then again, the Tatum style, once it appeared, never changed very much. There were no "periods" in his career for analysts to argue about, although the embellishments became slightly more lavish towards the end. So what we wind up with is a career packed with lack of incident, leaving the frustrated commentator only the actual music to talk about.

At which point the situation changes from difficult to impossible. There is no way of analysing the content of Tatum's playing which is not in the end self-defeating. Every sentence ever written about Tatum's music, every evaluation of one of his solos, every puff for one of his albums, is nothing more than proof of the old proposition that if it were really possible to describe the sound of music in words, then there would be no need to listen to it. The best anyone can do is to make a few points about those aspects of Tatum's jazz which have caused him sometimes to be neglected, or underrated, or even on occasions to be dismissed altogether; and to try to find out of what component parts Tatum's style is composed.

In approaching this area, we have to remember that for the most part jazz criticism has been conducted by those whose passionate love of the music was never quite passionate enough for them to learn the rudiments of jazzmaking, which means that when a player like Tatum puts his genius and his vast experience into a thirty-two bar chorus, it would be foolhardy to expect the average commentator to have the remotest idea what is going on. This explains why for many years there was a sizeable body of jazz critical opinion which dismissed Tatum as a jazz pianist altogether, and refused to admit his qualifications to be counted among such rivals as,

195

say, Jess Stacy or Bob Zurke. (I am casting no aspersions on
the playing of either Stacy or Zurke, but merely making the
point that to a critic who can only count up to four, the piano
playing he will find the most appealing will be the type of
piano playing mastered by players like Stacy and Zurke, and
that the inevitable result of this preference will be the mis-
taken impression that unless you play that way, you are not
playing jazz. Absurd, certainly, but it is exactly what happened to Tatum's reputation.)

The problem always was Tatum's frightening mastery of
Time, and his ability to subdivide it into the most deceptive
segments. In the recordings to which this essay is a hopeful
introduction, the listener will no doubt find time and time
again that there comes a moment when he loses his grasp
on the pulse of what Tatum is doing, that in tapping his foot,
either mentally or physically, the beat seems to have evaporated. At such moments, the disorientated listener, having
lost all sense of polarity as it were, can only sit there and
await the return of the familiar pulse he knows, and almost
every time that pulse comes back to him, it is either a split
second later or a split second earlier than he expected. The
explanation is quite simple. Tatum has been sliding imperceptibly from triplets to semi-quavers, or from semi-quavers
to grace notes, which are of course not part of the complement of the bar in which they occur, but embellishments of
that complement. When these moments occur the situation
is crystal-clear. The beat has gone, and that means that somebody has made a mistake. Either Tatum or the listener has
lost his way, and it is a tribute to the enormity of the old-time
jazz critic's pretensions to omniscience that he always insisted
that it was Tatum who was wrong. Thus there grew up the
canard that Tatum was not able to hold a tempo.

There was always a way out of this dilemma, and you may
ask why the confused critic did not take it. The answer is
that the solution lay in recourse to that invaluable invention,
the Metronome, a tiny machine which sets and maintains any

one tempo with a rigidity that only some mad scientist could ever have achieved. However, the chances are that when a man is so ignorant as to assume that he knows more about the pulse of a musical performance than Art Tatum does, then he will also be too ignorant ever to have heard of such a machine as a Metronome. The interesting thing is that when the so-called ramblings of Tatum at his most rococo are tested by the metronome, Tatum is found right every time. The rumour that Tatum couldn't maintain a tempo was a piece of imbecility which may safely be discounted in any serious discussion of his art.

What of his style in terms of jazz history? Whose influences flicker across the landscape of a Tatum solo? Who played Bechet to his Hodges, Oliver to his Armstrong, Hawkins to his Webster? The answer to these questions is, embarrassingly, everyone and no-one. Tatum has been the only soloist in jazz history to date who has made an attempt to conceive a style based on all styles, to master the mannerisms of all schools and then synthesise them into something personal. Obviously such a heroic concept requires miraculous technical mastery, which Tatum has. It also requires a complete understanding of what other players have been trying to do, which Tatum has. It requires an aesthetic morality compounded of courage and imagination, which Tatum has. Above all, it requires the ability to see the whole of jazz piano development in a single all-embracing context, an ability which Tatum has. (The exact parallel to this kind of eclecticism is James Joyce's *Ulysses* where, in the chapter entitled "The Oxen of the Sun," the writer offers perfect facsimiles of succeeding styles in English Literature, going from Anglo-Saxon infelicities, through Malory, Sir Thomas Browne, Bunyan, Pepys, Swift, Addison, Sterne and so on).

In a desperate attempt to follow Tatum through the labyrinth of his own reflections on style in jazz, let us concentrate for a moment on three of Tatum's greatest contemporaries at various stages of his journey, three men whose piano play-

ing unquestionably changed the face of jazz, and whose originality is beyond reasonable argument, let us say James P.
Johnson, Earl Hines and Bud Powell. James P. was the
founding father of a school of jazz piano known as "Stride"
because of the broad span required of a player's hands, which
created the illusion when you watched them instead of listening, of a man striding along a road. The Stride style remains interesting long after the world which nurtured it has
faded away, because of the striking imbalance achieved by
players like Johnson, between the three component parts of
music, Melody, Harmony and Rhythm. In the Stride school,
melody is to some extent sacrificed at the altar of harmonic
and rhythmic expediency. The Stride school was composed
of men like Johnson who spent a great part of their lives
playing unaccompanied in environments where nobody could
afford a large band, or even a rhythm section, so that the
Stride pianist had to have a left hand like a built-in rhythm
section, and a right hand which would not only play the tune
but also define the harmonic texture of that tune. The result
was an intriguing musical style in which the melody was always there but never quite defined, like a fish constantly
threatening to come to the surface but always remaining just
under the curl of the wave. (Paradoxically, both the elder
statesman of Stride piano James P, and his two most gifted
pupils, Duke Ellington and Thomas "Fats" Waller, were past
masters at the elusive art of writing commercial tunes. The
prowess of Duke and Fats in this regard is too well known
to need any amplification here, but it is sometimes forgotten
that Johnson too, wrote some of the best standard songs of
his era, including "Running Wild" and "If I Could Be With
You.")

The player who invented a new style to supersede Stride,
or at least the man who evangelised on behalf of the new style,
was Earl Hines. (The extent to which he invented the new
style or borrowed it from Teddy Weatherford is problematic
and of no vital importance in this context.) Hines conceived

the idea of using the right hand to play single-note improvisations based upon the chords, in contrast to the Stride pianists who were using their right hands to define the chords themselves. To clarify this distinction, let us say that a saxophonist faced with the challenge of playing on his instrument what James P. or Thomas Fats was playing in the right hand, would admit defeat as quickly as an octopus faced with the prospect of a pair of spectacles, and for the same reason. The saxophone, or the trumpet or the clarinet or any other instrument which is able to produce only one note at a time, cannot, by the very nature of its mechanics, play what a Stride pianist plays because the Stride pianist is playing ten notes at any one time. Hines introduced the antithesis to Stride playing, and it came to be called "Trumpet-style" piano, because the right hand of the pianist played single-note lines which might easily have been transcribed from a Louis Armstrong solo. (The interplay between Hines and Armstrong on their famous recording of "Weather Bird" marks one of the great moments of stylistic departure in jazz history.)

When a new age of Modernism arrived in the 1940s it was clear that of the two piano styles, it was Trumpet-style which was to dominate. In any case through the 1930s the Hines school had come into its own, for while the school of James P. was slowly petering out in imitations of imitations (James P. taught Waller who taught Joe Sullivan who influenced Jess Stacy, etc.), the Hines approach carried all before it, and even produced players influenced by Hines who were thought by many to have become better than their master. (Hines inspired Teddy Wilson, who invented Mel Powell, and so on.) The modern style rejoiced in a soloist like Bud Powell who, like Hines before him, was creating right-hand figures which echoed the solos of the great horn-players, except of course that where Hines had followed Armstrong, Powell was calling to mind Charlie Parker. But Powell was different in kind from Hines for another reason. He was thinking in a harmonic dimension quite different from the world through which Hines

199

had moved with such insolent ease. Powell was a child of the
generation that discovered the delights of chromatic thinking,
that took hold of the genial sequences of the Swing Age and
altered them almost beyond recognition. Powell and his con-
tempories were deploying the methods of Hines to express
the ideas of Parker, and the result was a style of piano playing
eons removed from Hines, both for its harmonic intricacy and
for the subtle amendments in rhythmic stress.

The reader may be pardoned for wondering at this stage
what Johnson, Hines and Powell have to do with Art Tatum.
The answer is that in Tatum's playing are incorporated the
very essence of the Stride School's great thumping tirades,
the very essence of the incandescence of Hines' right hand,
the very essence of Powell's harmonic sophistication. To put
it another way, Johnson, Hines and Powell were three men
who each achieved the colossal feat of amending the aesthetic
of jazz piano; Tatum achieved the even more colossal feat
of demonstrating that it was possible to master all three
styles, to flit from one to another within the space of a few
bars, and to blend these disparate elements into a coherent,
codified style by imposing on those elements the mark of his
own personality.

In Tatum's piano playing jazz finds its ultimate pianistic
expression, a piano style incorporating mastery of all piano
styles, just as in literature the English language found its ultimate verbal expression in James Joyce, whose prose style
was composed of the elements of all prose styles. What is
utterly fascinating about Tatum is that once having mastered
the various ways of playing jazz piano, he then showed how,
by switching from one to another in midthought, he could
express a style of his own. So many examples of this exist
that there is neither time nor space or purpose in listing
them, but a single example will surely be sufficient to make
the point. In "Lover Come Back to Me" Tatum repeatedly
returns to a leisurely, Johnsonian statement of Romberg's
melody after flirting with more baroque thoughts; the effect

of this switch from the ingenious to the ingenuous and back again to the ingenious may be taken as an identifying feature of Tatum's art. It is for this reason that his technique enabled him, not just to confuse listeners looking for a too-obvious statement of tempo, but also to define the elements of those styles which might have been thought to be antipathetic to him that even his most gifted contemporaries were flabbergasted by his jazz. One of his closest musical friends, Roy Eldridge, has described how, the first time Tatum appeared in a club where nobody was aware of this ability, "everybody stop playing." Such testaments proliferate through jazz history. Tatum shattered everyone; Tatum caused all the other musicians to lose confidence; Tatum terrified those who thought they knew how far jazz could be taken; and so on. It all reads like a first draft for a B-picture, and we would be inclined to reject it on those grounds were it not for the fact that the irrefutable evidence, the actual music, bears out everything the idolaters have ever said about Tatum.

Why, then, has there been so little analytical discussion of Tatum's music? After all, Coleman Hawkins' great solos have been transcribed; Bix Beiderbecke's fingerings have been written about with a solemnity that would have fractured Bix; you can buy a book of Earl Hines' fifty best hot licks; Louis Armstrong's solos have been put together and then taken apart again by every quack and every hack who ever enjoyed a Bunk Johnson performance; even the beautiful butterfly of Duke Ellington's orchestral technique has many times been broken on the wheel of textual investigation. Why, then, virtually nothing about the way Tatum goes about his business? The answer incorporates one of the best jokes in jazz history. The reason why nobody has tackled Tatum on this level is that nobody has been able to. Tatum is so good that he has daunted everybody. The jazz world has been too idle or too dumb to tackle so vast a project. Indeed, it is one of the great scandals of jazz history that while almost every major style has been given detailed attention, Tatum's remains an enigma, and for as long as this remains true, then jazz criticism will not be in a state of grace.

But Excalibur with nothing to cleave is a mere encumbrance. Having developed the greatest technique and the subtlest improvising mind in jazz, what is there on which the virtuoso may express it? Some creative artists of genius who find themselves delivered by circumstance into a world incapable of providing them with work to do commensurate with their abilities, provide their own, creating form as well as content. Liszt concocted keyboard problems worthy of his own technical mastery; Aeschylus, no doubt distracted by the voices he heard in his imagination, invented dialogue. Bernard Shaw not only perfected the discussion-drama but actually created performers to act it and audiences to applaud it. But Tatum could only have done something comparable by being a composer of appropriate themes at least fifty times as prolific as Gershwin, Porter, Berlin, Kern and Rodgers put together. For the jazz pianist might easily run through the entire life-work of a gifted songwriter in the course of single night's work, so how could he be expected to create a repertoire of his own songs vast enough to contain his own muse? Even Duke Ellington, who was the nearest thing to a bottomless pit of compositional melodic resource, was occasionally obliged to draw on the resources of other composers. Tatum found his own way round this problem, and it was a way which reveals one of the basic facts of the jazz life, a fact so obvious that we never even notice it, any more that we notice the taste of saliva in our own mouths.

And yet this one simple fact, which we take so much for granted that its implications are lost to us, is so extraordinary that there is surely no other kind of creative artist in any other line of business who would consider its restrictive effects compatible with the production of the highest quality work. It is as though a ballet company were required to please its audiences without benefit of Chopin or Tchaikovsky or Ravel or Stravinsky, or if Joe Louis had been asked to prove his mastery without the convenience of boxing rings, or Shakespeare expected to produce the plays without the existence of any English history. For the truth is that the jazz musician alone among the creative artists of our epoch has no repertoire which has been manufactured with his art in mind. So far as the jazz improvisor is concerned, no repertoire of his own has ever existed, so that a player like Tatum is placed in the situation of, say, a great concert piano virtuoso abroad in a world which has not yet evolved the delights of the concerto. Of course there is always the Blues, but a man cannot improvise on the same chord sequence all his life. So what is the jazz soloist to do? The answer is provided the moment we nominate the other favourite chord sequence of the jazz musician, the one usually named as being second only to the Blues in its general usefulness to the improvisor. That sequence is "I Got Rhythm," at which point we are witnesses to the most spectacular collision of two autonomous musical cultures.

We know, for example, that the Blues is genuine American Folk music in the sense that it arose and evolved through the vital needs of a social group. (When Ferdinand Jelly Roll Morton confessed "I did not invent the Blues," it was one of the very rare occasions on which he was telling the plain, unvarnished truth. Nobody invented the Blues because everybody invented them.) But when we turn to "I Got Rhythm," we are flung into a world that is highly artificial in the sense that the creative minds which adorn it are ultra-sophisticated, highly-trained, commercially-obligated, technically-refined. And most important of all, for the most part unconcerned with and sometimes totally ignorant of jazz, at times even violently antipathetic towards it, witness the attempts from time to time of distinguished popular composers to ban the issue of jazz recordings which distort the written melody. And yet it is this world which, inadvertently perhaps, provided jazz with its raw material, its thematic resources.

The comical incongruity of all this is demonstrated by the bare facts about "I Got Rhythm," which was first introduced to American audiences on October 14, 1930 at the Alvin Theatre, when a Miss Ethel Merman sang the words and music provided for her by George and Ira Gershwin. The show was called *Girl Crazy*, and its plot, a rambling farrago involving a dude ranch and lots of chorus girls, need not concern us here, except to make the point that the sheer irrelevance of these facts is an impressive testimony to the watchfulness of the jazz musician when it comes to finding suitable songs to play. (*Girl Crazy* was perhaps a special case in this regard, for its pit orchestra was not uncharacteristically packed with jazz musicians like Benny Goodman, Gene Krupa and Charlie Teagarden, who no doubt spread the word regarding the suitability of "I Got Rhythm" for jazz improvisation.)

It so happens that the American musical theatre enjoyed a golden age so far as melodic invention was concerned, and that this golden age coincided roughly with the professional lifespan of an artist like Tatum. Specific dates must always be arbitrary, but it is not altogether misleading to suggest that this great period began with the publication of Jerome Kern's "They Didn't Believe Me" in 1914 and ended after Irving Berlin shot his bolt, most brilliantly, by the way, with *Call Me Madam* in 1950. Why such golden ages occur is difficult, perhaps impossible to say, but certainly one of the more potent factors was the imbecility of the Romanov dynasty, which obligingly flung into the arms of American culture the families of George Gerswhin and Irving Berlin. Another factor must have been the comparative lowness of Broadway production costs, which made the gambling with untried talent a less terrifying affair than it later became. Undoubtedly a third factor was the pervading influence of jazz music on American culture generally, even though many of the songwriters who benefited remained all their lives in total ignorance of what had happened to them. Of course, not all the great composers of Broadway were unaware of what the jazz musician could do with their raw material, and it is perhaps aesthetic justice that the greatest of all these composers should have acknowledged the mastery of the greatest of these jazz musicians. In Oscar Levant's *A Smattering Of Ignorance* we read: "Despite his increasing interest in formal music and its background, Gerswhin never lost his love for dance music. The emergence of the swing phenomenon interested but did not surprise him, for such eminent performers as Benny Goodman, Gene Krupa, Red Nichols, Jack Teagarden, Jimmy Dorsey, Babe Rusin and Glenn Miller had contributed to the gaiety of *Strike Up the Band* and *Girl Crazy* as members of the pit orchestra. The Goodman Trio's record of 'Lady Be Good' delighted him, and he listened with rapture to Art Tatum (the great blind Negro pianist), especially to his playing of 'Liza' and 'I Got Rhythm'. He was so enthused with Tatum's playing that he had an evening for him at his 72nd Street apartment before leaving for Hollywood. Among George's invited guests was Leopold Godowsky, who listened with amazement for twenty minutes to Tatum's remarkable runs, embroideries, counter-figures and passage playing. The succeeding hour and a half of the same thing bored him, however. Some time after he arrived in California Gershwin discovered that Tatum was playing at a local nightclub, and we went together to hear him. It was a small, dingy, badly lighted room—an intimate version of the too-intimate Onyx Club. We joined the group of enthusiasts clustered around the piano where the blind virtuoso was in full swing. To George's great joy, Tatum played virtually the equivalent of Beethoven's thirty two variations on his tune 'Liza'. Then George asked for more."

Why should a musician like Art Tatum have found a song like "Liza" so intriguing? After all, it had been written as part of an indifferent backstage musical none of whose protagonists (apart from Gershwin himself) knew or cared a fig for musicians of Tatum's stamp. The answer to that question—indeed the answer to the question, Why the intimate relationship between the commercial theatre and an art-for-art's-sake music like jazz—consists of a single word; that word is Harmony.

To explain; what is jazz music, just how is it made? The improvisor takes a theme, states its melody briefly, and then creates fresh melodic lines based on the harmonies of the original melody. It becomes obvious that the lifeblood of the jazz musician is harmony; or rather combinations and sequences of harmony which engage his creative attention, those sequences which suggest to him certain new melodic patterns, sequences which mysteriously possess their own rhythmic dynamic, sequences whose ingenious convolutions help the improvisor not to repeat himself. And Tatum's whole generation stumbled on the truth that whether or not the tunesmiths of Broadway cared, they were turning out sequence after sequence of this kind, so that when the other circumstances of the successful musical had fallen away and been forgotten, when all the tinsel had gone back in the wardrobe and the crows' feet were treading all over the faces of once-beautiful leading ladies, when the jokes in the dialogue had long been left for dead and the thunderous hoofbeats of the chorus girls no longer reverberated to the back of the gallery, a residue was left behind, a residue of pure gold—the songs.

It is yet another irony of the history of twentieth-century music that it should have been the songs, which were at the time considered the least important items in the musical theatre, less vital than the drawing power of the star, less commercial than the style of the costumes, less respected than the libretto, should eventually have given the American musical comedy its only lasting element. Perhaps no more need be said about the interaction of the debt between the jazz soloist and the musical comedy writer than that out of the 179 sides which Art Tatum cut for Norman Granz, no fewer than 44 of them involved the work of the five major songwriters of the Golden Age, Gershwin, Berlin, Porter, Rodgers, and Kern, and that if we extend the list to include five other masters almost as accomplished, Walter Donaldson, Vincent Youmans, Harold Arlen, Duke Ellington, and Kurt Weill, the total goes up to 70. (These figures become even more impressive when we remember that most of the other themes come from Tin Pan Alley, whose songwriting methods were identical to those of Broadway, at least in the sense that qualitatively, there is little to choose between, say, "Dancing in the Dark" which comes from the musical stage, "Too Marvellous for Words" which comes from the musical cinema, and "Cherokee," which is just a song; the Golden Age was all-pervading.)

It is a piquant experience, this savouring of the accidental meeting of two cultures, this unpredictable romance between the contrivance of musical theatre and the tough, uncompromising, proudly uncommercial world of the jazz soloist. But mere piquancy would not be enough, I think, to justify any lengthy analysis. The most important thing of all to be said, not only about Tatum's jazz on these amazing sides, but also about the nature of his repertoire, is that, unbelievably, all these songs achieved their apotheosis, not at the hands of those artists for whom they were originally designed, but through the gifts of men like Tatum, who perhaps never sat through a musical comedy in his life. If "Liza" survives as a fragment of twentieth-century musical art, who will Gershwin have to thank, Ruby Keeler or Art Tatum? If "There'll Never Be Another You" survives long enough to commend its neat harmonic structure to the musicologists of the twenty-first century, who can Harry Warren thank for that, Sonja Henie or the generation of jazzmen who explored its potential? One sometimes wonders if George Gershwin ever knew that the most affecting vocal version of "Summertime," and perhaps the most original in concept, was Billie Holiday's.

Now it so happens that this whole area generally covered by the generic phrase, "show-tunes," has been shockingly badly documented, almost never annotated, never anthologised. The student who thinks that sheer artistic merit is enough to guar-

207

antee the survival of a song is advised to try buying the sheet music of "Stay As Sweet as You Are" or "That Old Feeling" and see how far he gets. It seems to me unarguable that the survival of such items is important, because a great deal of what is best in twentieth-century popular music is contained in items of that kind. A great many of the men who composed them were artistically feckless, some of them were shameless moneygrubbers, a few were pretentious popinjays, and some of them were so blinkered musically that they actually hated jazz. None of this has any relevance; all that matters is that this body of men produced a repertoire of songs so witty, so skilfully wrought, so finely finished, that it demands the talent of an Art Tatum to do it justice.

Such arrangements never come about. When has a great jazz virtuoso ever been invited into a studio and asked to play nearly two hundred songs of his choice the way he wants, sometimes even playing the same item twice if he believes, as is often the case, that a different tempo will reveal a different song? That is why the Art Tatum marathon is unique as well as vitally important for our understanding of two cultures, that of Broadway and that of the jazz musician. What Tatum did smacks of real genius. He sat at the piano and, drawing on a lifetime's experience in the smoky club-rooms of his youth, the days as a solo attraction and a trio leader, as a concert artist and a legend, he drew out from the stockroom of his recollection the songs that America had sung and danced to for the last thirty years. Of course he had no such intention in mind. But posterity must draw its conclusions from what the artist did, not what he thought he was doing, or meant to do, or felt he ought to do. Time and again in this remarkable collection of the finest piano solos ever made, the listener is pulled up short and his attention distracted for a moment by the sheer loveliness of the theme. Sometimes the tempo may surprise him, sometimes the drastic restructuring of the harmonic base may disconcert him; occasionally even the choice of theme will catch him unawares. But never will he find himself wondering why Tatum should have allowed into his pantheon an inferior theme, for in this collection there are no inferior themes.

A final reflection on how to listen to so vast an oeuvre of improvised music from a single voice. I remember back in the 1950s a friend of mine, a professional musician, acquired four of the Tatum solo albums, and finally came to the same conclusion that Mr. Godowsky does in Oscar Levant's memoir, namely that twenty minutes of Tatum is enough for any man. Mr Godowsky was quite wrong and so was my friend, who would certainly have reached a similar conclusion had he attempted to read ten Shakespeare plays in a day, or tried to mug up on all four Brahms symphonies at once. (I am not suggesting that Tatum is to be measured against Shakespeare or Brahms, but merely trying to point out that whatever the level of aesthetic power, there is such a thing as indigestion of the appreciative faculty.) Anyone who attempts to digest hours and hours of Tatum solo piano at a sitting is not only living his life the wrong way, but is also spoiling a great many pleasures which belong to tomorrow. Personal habits vary enormously, of course, and I can only report my own experiences with Tatum, without suggesting for a moment that they will be the same as anyone else's. (If anything I am unusually slow in building a close acquaintanceship with a great jazz performance.) After two months I found I could remember my way around some of the solo sides. After three months I was beginning to prefer some to others, always a good sign that understanding is flowering. After four months, I began to be able to name the titles even when switching on the middle of a moment of inspired fantasia on Tatum's part. After six months I sat down to compose these few reflections of one of the great recording events in the musical history of our time.

I would have liked longer, say another six months, but I suspect that even then I would still have wanted more time. For Tatum's art reveals more and more as one's study of it continues. My experience has been that first it discloses the nature of the instrument, then the nature of the material, then the nature of the musician. And then, ultimately, the nature of the listener. I know now, after living with Tatum's music for a time, that it was foolhardy of me ever to have become an instrumentalist myself.